"Improvement in the Management and Trade of the State Canals."

PROCEEDINGS

OF THE

STATE CANAL CONVENTION,

HELD AT

ROCHESTER, JANUARY 19TH, 1870.

CONVENTION CALLED BY THE
COMMERCIAL UNION OF THE STATE OF NEW-YORK.

NEW-YORK:
GEORGE F. NESBITT & CO., PRINTERS,
Corner Pearl and Pine Streets.

1870.

"Improvement in the Management and Trade of the State Canals."

PROCEEDINGS

OF THE

STATE CONVENTION,

HELD AT

ROCHESTER, JANUARY 19TH, 1870,

TO CONSIDER MEASURES FOR REFORMING THE MANAGEMENT AND IMPROVING THE TRADE OF THE NEW-YORK STATE CANALS.

CONVENTION CALLED BY THE
COMMERCIAL UNION OF THE STATE OF NEW-YORK.

New-York:
GEORGE F. NESBITT & CO., PRINTERS AND STATIONERS,
CORNER OF PEARL AND PINE STREETS.
1870.

INDEX.

	PAGES.
ALLEN, WM. F., Letter from,	25
APPENDIX,	83
BUSINESS of the Convention,	41
BROOKS, ERASTUS, Free Canals,	97
CONVENTION at Rochester, Call for,	3
" " Proceedings,	19
" " Resolutions at,	42, 43, 79, 80
" " Committees of,	25
CAMPBELL, DR., Prayer by,	19
COOPER, PETER, Letter from,	27
CHAMBER OF COMMERCE, Letter from,	32
CITIZENS' ASSOCIATION, Letter from,	27
COMMITTEE on Resolutions,	25
" " Business,	25
CONNOLLY, RICH'D B., Letter from,	26
CANAL APPRAISERS, Resolution as to,	79
COURT OF CLAIMS,	79
COMMON COUNCIL of Rochester,	6, 79
" " Buffalo,	7
CONTRACT SYSTEM,	29, 41, 42, 55, 64, &c.
COMSTOCK, GEO. F., Opinion by,	98
DALY, JOSEPH F., Secretary of Convention,	24
DELEGATES to Rochester Convention,	5 to 18
DODGE, WM. E., Letter from,	32
DAVIS, E. E., Speech of,	55
EVARTS, WM. M., Opinion by,	99
FISH, HENRY L., Speech of,	59
FUNDING STATE DEBT,	43, 47, 98, 110
GANSON, JOHN, Opinion,	98
HATCH, ISRAEL T., Speech by,	43
KING, CHARLES A., Speech of,	75
LORD, JARVIS D., Letter from,	64
MITCHELL, DAVID J., Speech by,	70
MOULTON, FRANCIS D., Speech by,	100
NILES, HIRAM, Speech of,	87
NICHOLS, ASHER P., Letter,	28
PARSONS, THOMAS, Letter from,	33
PRODUCE EXCHANGE, Proceedings,	85
PORTER, JOHN K., Opinion by,	98
RESOLUTIONS of Convention,	42, 43, 79, 80
REPAIRS OF CANALS,	29, 41, 42, 43, 55, 64, &c.
SANDS, NATHANIEL, President of Convention,	20
" " Speeches by,	20, 80
SEYMOUR, HORATIO, Speech by,	35
SECRETARY of Convention and Assistants,	24
STANFORD, CHARLES, Speech by,	65
STATISTICS of Tonnage and Freight,	101
TOLEDO, City of, Delegation,	11, 75
TONNAGE DUES on Canal Boats,	79
TOLLS, Reduction of,	37, 87
VICE-PRESIDENTS of Convention,	23, 24
WALKER, ELMORE, Statistics by,	100, 101, &c.

CALL FOR THE CONVENTION.

COMMERCIAL UNION

OF THE STATE OF NEW-YORK,

813 BROADWAY,

NEW-YORK, *December 30th*, 1869.

You are invited to attend a General Convention of the COMMERCIAL UNION, to be held at Corinthian Hall, in the City of Rochester, on Wednesday, January 19th, 1870, at 10 o'clock A. M., to consider the subject of Reforming the Official Management and Improving the Trade of the Canals of the State of New-York.

Yours, respectfully,

State Central Committee of the Commercial Union.
{
NATHANIEL SANDS, New-York, PRES'T.,
HENRY L. FISH, Rochester,
M. M. CALEB, New-York,
NILES CASE, Buffalo,
JEREMIAH P. ROBINSON, New-York,
EDWARD HINCKEN, New-York,
CHENEY AMES, Oswego,
L. J. N. STARK, New-York,
JOSEPH F. DALY, New-York, SEC'Y.

DELEGATES

TO THE
CONVENTION CALLED BY THE COMMERCIAL UNION
AT ROCHESTER, JANUARY 19TH, 1870.

State Central Committee of the Commercial Union.

NATHANIEL SANDS,	NEW-YORK,	*President*,
M. M. CALEB,	"	
L. J. N. STARK,	"	
JEREMIAH P. ROBINSON,	"	*Treasurer*,
EDWARD HINCKEN,	"	
HENRY L. FISH,	ROCHESTER,	
NILES CASE,	BUFFALO,	
CHENEY AMES,	OSWEGO,	
JOSEPH F. DALY,	NEW-YORK,	*Secretary*.

NEW-YORK CITY DELEGATES.

S. D. HARRISON,
L. HAZELTINE,
ALEX. E. ORR,
ADON SMITH,
C. PARISH,
S. K. LANE,
A. E. MASTERS,
R. H. LAIMBEER,
HENRY BUELL,
JESSE HOYT,
DAVID DOWS,
J. M. FISKE,
J. H. HERRICK,
E. W. COLEMAN,
CARLOS COBB,
E. S. BROWN,
L. B. SHAW,
W. B. BARBER,
U. C. WHITLOCK,
FRANCIS D. MOULTON,
GEORGE W. SMITH,
E. H. TOMPKINS,

A. R. GRAY,
L. J. N. STARK,
WM. H. POWER,
MILTON KNAPP,
A. F. ROBERTS,
ROBERT P. GETTY,
R. B. MINTURN,
G. A. BRETT,
J. W. ELWELL,
E. ANNANN,
M. M. CALEB,
A. S. JEWELL,
B. P. BAKER,
ARCHIBALD BAXTER,
BENJ. LOGAN,
G. D. CRAGIN,
J. S. WILLIAMS,
C. H. MARSHALL,
EDWARD HINCKEN,
J. M. BOYNTON,
GEORGE D. PUFFER,
F. EDSON.

ROCHESTER, Monroe County.

E. M. SMITH, *Mayor of Rochester*,
THOMAS PARSONS,
S. M. SPENCER,
B. SPENCER,
JOSEPH H. POOL,
JOHN WILLIAMS,
CHARLES F. SMITH,
W. F. HOLMES,
S. B. RAYMOND,
EZRA R. ANDREWS,
A. G. WHITCOMB,
C. R. PARSONS,
JAMES BRACKET,
L. C. SPENCER,
H. C. WEBSTER,
N. D. ENSIGN,
DANIEL COTTER,
HENRY SHAFFER,
JOHN BIRD,
JACOB MEYER,
HENRY L. FISH,
JAMES E. CONLON,
SAMUEL STODDARD,
P. B. WHITBECK,
EDWARD BACKUS,
GEORGE J WHITNEY,
CHARLES B. HILL,
JAMES M. WHITNEY,
G. H. BURBANK,
M. F. REYNOLDS,
GEO. C. BUELL,
W. A. REYNOLDS,
C. E. UPTON,
CHARLES A. JEFFORDS,
WILLIAM AIKENHEAD,
W. S. THOMPSON,
G. H. PERKINS,
HENRY B. KNAPP,
JOHN S. DRAKE,
C. W. HASBROUCK,
C. C. MEYER,
ROBERT BARRETT,
HENRY SPOOR,
JEROME BARHYDT,
TOWNSEND W. SMITH,
WM. W. FURMAN,
WM. PUNCH,
JOHN CONNER,
HAMILTON McQUATTERS,
JEROME HATHAWAY,
JOSEPH ENSIGN,
H. W. RICH,
RUFUS TERRY,
P. J. MEYER,
ELDRIDGE HEATH,
DANIEL H. BROMLEY,
NATHANIEL THOMPSON,
THERON E. PARSONS,
GEO. B. SHAFFER,
HUGH BLAIR,
A. J. PALMER,
THOMAS CARROLL,
N. B. ELLISON,
GEO. W. PARSONS,
AMBROSE CRAM,
STEPHEN REMINGTON,

THE COMMON COUNCIL OF THE CITY OF ROCHESTER.

ALBANY, Albany County.

O. L. HASCY,
L. THOMSON,
C. A. SWEET,
C. P. EASTON,
S. G. CHASE.

ITHACA, Tompkins County.

WM. W. ESTY,
JOHN HAWKINS,
T. W. SEELY,
B. F. TABOR,
J. C. KING,
ABRAM VAN ORDER,
W. A. J. OZMUN,
CALVIN TICHENOR.

BUFFALO, Erie County.

THE MAYOR AND COMMON COUNCIL OF THE CITY OF BUFFALO,

S. S. GUTHRIE,
G. S. HAZARD,
A. NELSON,
J. S. MUNDERBACH,
WILLIAM PETRIE,
H. FILES,
P. H. BECKWITH,
E. GALLAGHER,
H. M. BARKER,
CHARLES A. SWEET,
J. L. GREENMAN,
JOHN H. VOUGHT,
HENRY MORSE,
E. S. J. BEMIS,
JOSEPH CARLEY,
JAMES VAN BUREN,
WILLIAM H. COBB,
N. HALL,
FRANK BEADLE,
A. W. HORTON,
JOHN B. MANNING,
JOHN BISSELL,
ROBERT BARNARD,
ARTHUR D. BISSELL,
J. M. MATTHEWS,
GEORGE SANDROCK,
C. F. STERNBERG,
EDWIN GILBERT,
WILLIAM J. MORGAN,
E. E. HAZARD,
O. G. STEELE, Jr,
CYRUS CLARK,
JAMES D. SAWYER,
WILLIAM THURSTONE,
A. P. WRIGHT,
THOMAS CHESTER,
A. S. CARPENTER,
ADAM HOMER,
J. SHAVER, Jr.,
B. F. BRUCE,
GEORGE D. PLIMPTON,
WILLIAM H. ABELL,
R. C. PALMER,
LAURENS ENOS,
R. COLLINS,
E. W. WILBER,
S. K. WORTHINGTON,
A. RICHMOND,
JOHN PEASE, Jr.,
JOHN PEASE,
NELSON BOSTWICK.

TONAWANDA, Erie County.

F. F. HOYER,
W. T. BRUSH,
H. B. RANSOM,
L. S. PAYNE,
S. G. JOHNSON,
V. SMITH,
H. NEWELL,
B. H. LONG,
S. A. VAN BROKLYN,
JOHN HUFF,
WILLIAM SCHROMGER,
PAUL ROBERTS,
B. H. NEFF,
B. F. FELTON,
A. B. WILLIAMS.

WEST TROY, Rensselaer County.

L. D. COLLINS,
HARRY FITCHETT,
GEORGE B. MOSHER,
J. HALSINGER,
JEFFERSON COLLINS,
T. CUMMINGS,
MATTHEW ROWE,
L. R. AVERY,
J. F. PHELPS,
D. W. TALCOTT,
S. H. WATERMAN,
O. F. POTTER,
A. J. RUSSELL,
R. J. GETTY.

SYRACUSE, Onondaga County.

J. P. HASKINS,
S. W. BARKER,
H. M. BANCROFT,
SILAS TITUS,
JOHN GREENWAY,
VIVUS W. SMITH,
JOHN M. STRONG,
CHARLES NICHOLS,
JOHN J. CROUSE,
EZRA DOWNER,
JOHN M. JAYCOX,
E. C. DODGE,
HENRY PRATT,
A. A. HOWLITT,
WILLIAM C. GAYE,
W. T. HAMILTON,
W. D. STEWART,
R. S. RAYMOND,
JOHN LIGHTON,
HARVEY STEWART,
H. H. FREEMAN,
J. J. GLASS,
JAMES JOHNSON,
W. G. SPRAGUE,
JACOB AMOS,
L. H. REDFIELD,
PHILIP P. MIDLER,
ASEL F. WILCOX,
DAVID J. MITCHELL.

CLYDE, Wayne County.

S. D. STREETER,
JOHN CROWELL,
CHARLES SMITH,
A. GRISWOLD,
WM. C. ELY,
JAMES STREETER,
J. VANDERBERG,
THOMAS P. THORN.

PALMYRA, Wayne County.

ELIJAH ENNIS,
C. J. FARRIN,
FRANKLIN LAKEY,
WILLIAM H. BOWMAN,
P. TUCKER,
J. W. CORNING,
E S. AVERILL,
JOSEPH E. COCHRAN,
MARVIN HILL,
JOHN F. STRAIN,
A. J. WALTON,
H. S. FLOWER,
LEMUEL DURFEE.

BROCKPORT, Monroe County.

JAMES H. WARREN,
HORACE J. THOMAS,
J. D. DECKER,
THOMAS CORNES,
WM. H. BUNN,
LUTHER GORDER,
R. M. PALMER.

OGDEN, Monroe County.

JOHN BORST,
EZEKIEL BROWN,
SAMUEL WHITTIER,
JOHN O. BARCLAY,
JOSIAH RICH,
WM. BARNARD,
ALLEN MARSHALL.

LOCKPORT, Niagara County.

A. A. BISSELL,
JASON COLLIER,
E. M. ROGERS,

H. S. PARMELEE,
H. F. CADY.

BRIGHTON, Monroe County.

S. P. GOULD,
B. W. FASSETT,
W. J. BABCOCK,

J. M. BABCOCK,
S. H. GOULD,
IRA TODD.

TROY, Rensselaer County.

PERRY E TOLES,
WILLIAM H. BEAMAN,
GEORGE C. BURDETT,

G. L. DOUGLAS,
JOHN L. BLANCHARD.

PORT GIBSON AND VICINITY, Ontario County.

L. C. RUSSELL,
S. T. STACY,
JOHN H. RUSSELL,
WM. H. BURGETT,
J. L. WILSON,
A. B. PEPER,
WM. BLOSSOM,
JAMES H. IRWIN,
LYMAN CLARK,

J. W. PARKER,
JOHN H. SCHUTT,
JOSEPH BLOSSOM,
A. T. GOLDSWORTH,
WM. S. WESTFALL,
HENRY BLOSSOM,
CHARLES E. PHELPS,
GEORGE S. SNYDER.

OSWEGO, Oswego County.

O. H. HASTINGS,
W. D. SMITH,
J. W. PITKIN,
W. H. WHEELER,
W. A. RUNDELL,
A. H. FAILING,
CHENEY AMES,
F. T. CARRINGTON,
B. HAGAMAN,
A. S. PAGE,
J. K. POST,

M. MERICK,
D. G. FORT,
W. H. HERRICK.
B. DOOLITTLE,
W. W. WRIGHT,
GEORGE B. SLOAN,
D. L. COUCH,
L. B. ROBE,
ALBERT F. SMITH,
E. M. FORT.

FAIRPORT, Monroe County.

T. L. HURLBURT,
SMITH WILBUR,
GEORGE B. FOSTER,

GEORGE SOSS,
W. K. GOODRICH.

UTICA, Oneida County.

J. E. B. THORN,	A. N. POMEROY,
A. E. CULVER,	J. H. MALLORY.

PHENIX, Oswego County.

JOSEPH GILBERT,	IRA BETTS.
T. E. GILBERT,	

ALBION, Orleans County.

GEORGE CLYDE,	EDWIN FARMER,
HERAM HARRIS,	THOMAS FOSTER.

HINDSBURGH, Orleans County.

JACOB HINDS,	CORNELIUS THOMAS.
L. W. BURNS,	JAMES BURNS.

PORTVILLE, Cattaraugus County.

JOHN G. MERSEREAU,	WALLACE W. WESTON,
B. S. COLWELL,	W. G. TRUESDELL,
WILLIAM F. WHEELER,	H. C. SCOFIELD.

FULTONVILLE, Montgomery County.

A. J. GATES,	WM. H. MEAD.

FORT EDWARD, Washington County.

D. UNDERWOOD,	GEORGE SATTERLEE.

WHITEHALL, Washington County.

E. E. DAVIS,	E. A. MARTIN,
H. R. SNYDER	W. H. TEFFT.

NEWARK, Wayne County.

D. A. SHERMAN,	H. H. MORSE,
RODNEY BOOTH,	DAVID TAMARANTH.

WATERFORD, Saratoga County.

JOHN TITCOMB,	J. B. ENOS.

GLENS FALLS, Warren County.

JOHN KEENAN,	D. PECK.

FORT ANN, Washington County.

DAVID RICE,	JOHN BARNARD

SANDY HILL, Washington County.
ORSON RICHARDS.

PORT HENRY, Essex County.
S. H. WITHERBEE.

SCHUYLERSVILLE, Essex Co.
SIDNEY SEELY, | GEORGE L. AMES.

ARGYLE, Washington County.
ALEXANDER BARCLAY.

FOREIGN DELEGATES.

TOLEDO, Ohio.

C. A. KING,
D. B. SMITH,
A. L. BACKUS,

E. WILLIAMS,
P. B. JOHNSON.

DELEGATES AT LARGE INVITED.

NEW-YORK.

A. OAKEY HALL, *Mayor of the City of New-York.*
HUGH ALLEN,
D. T. ALBERTSON,
EDWARD BILL,
H. H. BUCKBEE,
THOMAS J. CREAMER,
RICHARD B. CONNOLLY,
WM. H. FOGG,
WM. H. GUION,
JOHN HOBBS,
C. R. HICKOX,
ROBT. C. HUTCHINGS,
SAMUEL KNAPP,
MICHAEL NORTON,
A. H. PHILLIPS,
A. L. ROWE,
LEWIS ROBERTS,
HUGH SHOTWELL,
PETER B. SWEENY,
WM. M. TWEED,
FRANKLIN WOODRUFF,
C. C. WINANS,
SAML. WILLETTS,

JAMES P. WALLACE,
H. O. ARMOUR,
O. BREED,
W. W. BRUCE,
R. S. BROWN,
PETER COOPER,
J. W. EDDY,
THOS. W. GRIFFIN,
WM. H. HARRIS,
HARVEY E. HICKS,
A. M. HOYT,
STEPH. HENRY OLIN,
L. D. KIERNAN,
HENRY O'REILLY,
WALWORTH PATERSON,
J. C. ROWAN,
P. W. SPRAGUE,
J. V. SPADER,
PAUL N. SPOFFORD,
RICHARD M. HENRY,
GEORGE WADE,
HEMAN D. WALBRIDGE,
WILLIAM WOOD,
T. S. YOUNG.

ALBANY.

C. W. ARMSTRONG,
A. S. CLARKE,
THOMAS EARLY,
ASA FASSETT,
S. HALE,
JAMES HIGGINS,
P. H. HOLLIGAN,
J. N. KEELER,
SAMUEL KIRK,
JOHN LANE,
MICHAEL LYMAN,
D. D. C. MINK,
MINOS McGOWEN,
B. H. MILLS,
DANIEL O'KEEFE,
WM. PARK,
CHAS. B. REDFIELD,
P. RONAN,
CHAS. T. SHEPARD,
WM. H. TAYLOR,
F. W. VOSBURG,
EDWARD WHITNEY,

FRANK CHAMBERLAIN,
A. E. DURANT,
JOHN FULTON,
DAVID N. GLAZIER,
JAMES HENDRICK,
GILBERT HUNTER,
B. JUDGE,
THOS. KEARNEY,
W. LACY,
PETER LYONS,
S. McKISSICK,
PHILLIP MATTIMORE,
THOS. J. NEVILLE,
HIRAM PERRY,
D. PREST,
ALEX. ROBERTSON,
HENRY SMITH,
JOHN H. TROWBRIDGE,
H. S. VANZANTVOORD,
WM. H. WEAVER,
JOHN WARD.

PORT BYRON.

N. J. ARMSTRONG,
WM. N. HALSEY,
EDWIN HIEN,
SMITH D. MALLORY,
W. SITTSER,
ABRAHAM GUTCHESS,

WM. J. CORNELL,
D. E. HAVENS,
JOHN JONES,
GEO. W. PERKIN,
CHAS. H. WEED,
STEPHEN GUTCHESS.

MOUNT MORRIS.

C. B. ADAMS,
Col. J. BODINE,
JAMES R. BOND,
SAMUEL GALBRAITH,
H. W. MILLER,
H. P. MILLS,
JOHN VERNAM,
ELIJAH YOUNG,

Dr. G. W BRANCH,
H. E. BROWN,
NORMAN FOOT,
FRED. HASTINGS,
JACOB A. MEAD,
FRANK NORTHWAY,
CHAS. WINIGAR.

ANNSVILLE.

JAMES ARMSTRONG,
C. B. COVENTRY,
RICHARD G. SAVERY,

H. BECKER,
D. B. DANFORTH.

ROME.

E. B. ARMSTRONG,
ADDISON DAY,
N. B. FOOT,
GILES HAWLEY,
T. G. HALLEY,
ROBERT H. HUGHES,
F. W. OLIVER,
WM. PARKER,
HARRISON PEASE,
JAMES STEVENS,
HENRY W. TIBBITTS,
B. W. WILLIAMS,

JOHN J. BRADT,
A. ETHEREDGE,
JEROME GRAVES,
B. N. HUNTINGTON,
JOHN HOOK,
SAMUEL P. LEWIS,
WM. S PARKHURST,
HENRY W. PELL,
GEORGE P. RUSS,
G. V. SHELDON,
THOS. W. WILLIAMS,
HARRISON JACOBS.

VERONA.

JAMES L. ABELL,
WM. CLARK,
THOS. MULHALL,
E. P. ROBERTS,
E. C. STARKS,

W. H. BENNETT,
N. HALLIDAY,
R. PAIGE,
GEORGE H. SANDFORD,
S. P. SMITH.

SANDY HILL.

LORAIN ALLEN,
DAN. J. FINCH,
JAMES H. SHERRILL,
HENRY TEFFT,

WILLIAM COLEMAN,
HIRAM KENYON,
GEORGE B. SHERRILL,
A. HOLBROOK.

PALMYRA.

ORNON ARCHER,

JAMES PEDDIE.

BUFFALO.

JOHN ALLEN,
GEO. W. BULL,
Hon. J. G. BAMLER,
A. M. CLAPP,
M. R. EAMES,
A. L. GRIFFIN,
Hon. I. T. HATCH,
D. C. LITTLEJOHN,
J. S. NOYES,
O L. NIMS,
Hon. E. S. PROSSER,
LYMAN B. SMITH,
GEORGE R. WILSON,

D. S. BENNETT,
WM. H. BARCLAY,
JNO. A. B. CAMPBELL,
EDWIN T. EVANS,
Hon. RICH. FLACH,
ISAAC HOLLOWAY,
FRANK C. KING,
HIRAM NILES,
Hon. A. P. NICHOLS,
SOLOMON PARMELEE,
C. O. SHEPARD,
A. SWEET.

CHAMPLAIN.

J. M. BOWNE,

W. F. COOK.

NEW LONDON.

HOMER C. PAIGE,
ALEX. RAYNSFORD,
L. P. SMITH,

E. P. ROBERTS,
W. SWAN.

BROCKPORT.

H. A. BEECH,
A. D. GRAVES,
F. BRAINARD,

J. D. DECKER,
HENRY W. SEYMOUR.

ROCHESTER.

BENJAMIN BUTLER,
H. C. DANIELS,
GEORGE H. FORSTER,
JOHN McGRAU,
DUDLEY D. PALMER,
B. VAUGHN,

GEO. G. COOPER,
DR. W. M. FLEMING,
WM. GUGGENHEIM,
H. A. PALMER,
JOSEPH QUALTROUGH,
DANIEL WARNER.

LOCKPORT.

ROBT. DUNLAP,
BENJ. FARLEY,
G. D. LAMONT,
R. M. SKEELS,
ALFORD H. SMITH,
D. A. VAN VALKENBURG,

T. T. FLAGLER,
C. A. FOLGER,
S. ROGERS,
CHESTER F. SHELLEY,
URIAH TINN.

ILION.

DEAN BURGESS,
ROBERT ETHERIDGE,
E. W. STANNARD,
JOHN H. RAISBECK,
A. C. McGOWAN,

O. B. BEALS,
EZRA GRAVES,
JOSIAH SHULL,
A. H. PRESCOTT,
SAML. MORGAN.

LITTLE FALLS.

LEONARD BOYER,
CHAS. A. GIRVAN,

H. DERBY.

UTICA.

HORATIO SEYMOUR,
LEVI BLAKESLEE,
M. C. COMSTOCK,
CHARLES H. HOPKINS,
ISAAC WHIFFIN,

M. T. MEEKER,
DANIEL CROUNCE,
T. S. FAXTON,
N. KISSAM,
JAS. SAYRE.

SCHUYLERVILLE.

PETER J. COOKE,
H. HOLMES,
SAMUEL SHELDON,

RICHARD ENGLISH,
C. W. MAYHEW,
ALONSON WELCH.

JOHN BRICK,
STEPHEN COVILL,
WM. FALKNER,
H. McGALWAY,
HORACE WESTCOTT,

VIENNA.
ALLEN COVILL,
E. S. DOE,
JOHN A. HORN,
FREDERICK PETRIE.

FORT PLAIN.
WILLIAM CLARK, | A. MATHESON.

PORTVILLE.
GEO. CHAMBERLAIN, | L. SIMPSON.

BOONVILLE.
JOHN ANDERSON,
H. W. BENTLY,
SAMUEL FERGUSON,

ROBERT BAMBER,
L. COOK,
P. B. SCHULTZ.

SHEBURNE.
DEVILLO WHITE.

FORT ANN.
O. W. SHELDON.

SYRACUSE.
THOMAS G. ALVORD, | J. M. WIETING.

PORT GIBSON. | *MEDINA.*
JOHN SISSON. | JOHN JACKSON.

SANGERFIELD.
ALANSON B. CADY, | JAMES PRESTON.

ROTTERDAM. | *CAMILLUS.*
JOHN W. VEEDER. | DAVID ALLEN.

TROY.
GEO. BABCOCK,
G. L. DOUGLASS,
JOHN L. FLAGG,
J. M. FRANCIS,
J. U. FREEMAN,
THOS. McMANUS,
F. S. THAYER,
M. I. TOWNSEND,

THOS. COLEMAN,
CHAS. EDDY,
JOSEPH W. FULLER,
JAS. FORSYTH,
ROBERT GREEN,
P. A. MOORE.
C. U. TILLINGHAST,
R. D. SILLIMAN.

EAGLE HARBOR.
WILLIAM R. BIRD.

CAMDEN.

P. B. COSTELLO,
S. CROMWELL,
GEO. CARROLL,
THOS. D. PENFIELD.

WHITEHALL.

O. BASCOM,
GEORGE BRETT,
O. F. DAVIS,
N. T. JILLSON,
W. J. SMITH,
P. W. SCRIBNER,
SIDNEY BROWN,
TRACEY COWEN,
H. T. GAYLORD,
ORSON RICHARDS,
T. T. VAUGHAN.

GENEVA.

WM. CHIPPS,
W. L. GILBERT,
JOHN OSTRANDER,
J. K. CHIPPS,
RICHD. KNIGHT.

SENECA FALLS.

J. B. DANIELS,
GEO. HOYT,
J. SCHOONMAKER,
A. C. GIBBS,
G. HAIGHT,
G. WILCOXSON.

MECHANICSVILLE.
A. K. CORNELL.

FAIRPORT.
CHARLES BURLINGAME.

FULTONVILLE.

WM. CHATMAN,
J. R. PUTNAM,
F. FISH,
P. VAN ANTWERP,
A. J. YATES.

FLORENCE.

J. A. COWLES,
LEWIS RIDER.

CHITTENANGO.
ROBERT CURTIS.

MIDDLEPORT.
HENRY CORNES.

ALBION.

JOHN BERRY,
S. HARWOOD,
W. A. HOWARD,
WM. HARVER,
WALTER WAGER,
L. J. PECK,
DENNIS DENSMORE,
C. A. HARRINGTON,
PETER S. HARVER,
E. R. TANNER,
H. J. SICKLES.

WHITESTONE.

AMBROSE NICHOLS,
W. R. ROBBINS.

PRINCETOWN.
WILLIAM DOUGALL.

MACEDON.

L. DURFEE, | PETER THURSTON.

LEE.

JAY CAPRON, | W. F. FIELD.
ISAAC McDOUGALL, |

TICONDEROGA.

H. G. BURLEIGH, | GEORGE MARSHALL.

WATERFORD.

C. BREWSTER, | J. B. ENOS,
H. VANDENBURG, | C. VANDERCAN,
J. PRATT, | D. REED.
E. STEWART, |

WEST TROY.

JAMES E. CRAIG, | WM. A. FASSETT,
C. G. HILL, | T. W. JACKSON,
M. McDONOUGH, | C. D. ROUSSEAU,
JOHN RILEY, | A. W. RICHARDSON,
JAMES ROY, | PETER SAXE,
D. SCRAFFORD, | WM. D. SUNDERLIN.
C. K. TINNEY, |

CRESCENT.

C. SANFORD COWLES, | CHAS. H. CLUTE,
PHILLIP POTTS, | C. J. WARRINGTON.

OSWEGO.

C. M. JOHNSON, | GEO. B. POWELL,
CHESTER PENFIELD, | JOHN A. PLACE.
JOHN W. PRATT, | WM. F. ALLEN.

SCHENECTADY.

A. W. HUNTER, | J. HARRIS,
WM. H. HELMER, | G. G. MAXON,
ANDREW McMULLEN, | Hon. CHAS. STANFORD,
G. M. TIMBERMAN, | DANIEL VAN VRANKEN,

CLYDE.

Hon. L. S. KETCHUM, | J. M. NICHOLS.

HAMILTON.

W. T. MANCHESTER, | J. MASON,
N. WILSON PARKER, | D. B. WEST.

BALDWINSVILLE.

JAS. FRAZER, | W. L. WILKINS.

GLENVILLE.
A. Y. CARNER.

WATERLOO.
C. COLE.

ITHACA.
D. C. GARRITT, | JEROME NORTON.

KIRKLAND.
HENRY S. ARMSTRONG, | JAMES C. BRONSON

WESTPORT.
V. C. SPENCER.

PLATTSBURGH.
J. T. B. KETCHAM, | C. F. NORTON.
ANDREW WILLIAMS, |

LIVERPOOL.	*ROUSE'S POINT.*
LUCIUS GLEASON.	F. W. MYERS.
NEWARK.	*WEEDSPORT.*
JAS. D. FORD.	W. M. QUAGG.
DUANESBURGH.	*EATON.*
JAMES J. HARE.	ALPHEUS MORSE.
AVA.	*ELBRIDGE.*
SAML. HULBERT.	JAMES MONROE.
FAYETTEVILLE.	*GEORGETOWN.*
HIRAM EATON.	LINA J. MORSELY.
CANASTOTA.	*NORTHUMBERLAND.*
THOS. BARLOW.	S. LEWIS.
GLENS FALLS.	*DURHAMVILLE.*
Hon. H. R. WING.	JAMES JENNISON.
HULLERTON.	*WALWORTH.*
WM. M. YAGER.	ABNER NELSON.
FULTON.	
F. M. WILSON.	

WATKINS.
O. P. BOWER, | A. H. DAVIS,
F. DAVIS, Jr., | D. P. DEY,
JOHN LANG, | GEORGE J. MAGEE.
LORENZO WEBBER, |

PROCEEDINGS

OF

THE CONVENTION.

The Delegates met at Corinthian Hall, in the City of Rochester, on Wednesday, the 19th day of January, 1870, at 10 o'clock A. M., pursuant to call. The platform was occupied by the STATE CENTRAL COMMITTEE and Officers of the COMMERCIAL UNION, the MAYORS of the Cities of ROCHESTER and BUFFALO and the invited guests of the Convention, including Hon. HORATIO SEYMOUR.

The Delegates from the several cities, towns, villages, Boards of Trade and Associations mentioned in the foregoing pages filled the body of the Hall.

The Convention was called to order by the Hon. HENRY L. FISH of Rochester, who introduced the Rev. DOCTOR CAMPBELL of Rochester, who offered the following

PRAYER.

Almighty and everlasting God; to those of us who acknowledge Thee in all our ways, Thou hast promised that if we do so, Thou wilt direct our steps. In all great undertakings of life we need Thy blessing, and without that blessing it is impossible for us to secure permanent and desirable prosperity; therefore we invoke Thy blessing at the present time, and upon the undertaking of the present occasion. Bestow upon us the light of Thy countenance, and grant to us that wisdom that comes down from Heaven.

All the great interests of government, all the interests of commerce, all we effect, whether favorable or unfavorable to our social relations, is under Thy control and in Thy hands; and Thy blessings we beseech in whatever shall be done. And we pray that in this great State those who direct the administration of its affairs may be under Thy divine guidance and direction.

We pray that Thou wilt guide the members of this Convention this day in their deliberations, and give them wisdom to conduct the great interests they are met here to protect: and that Thou wilt make the work of their hands in this great cause successful, and strengthen them to achieve the worthy purposes they have in view.

We pray that wickedness, and corruption, and crime, in whatever form they present themselves, and in whatever guise they take, may be eradicated in this country, and in this State, and may be removed far from us, and that righteousness, justice and peace may triumph everywhere. Command Thy blessing upon the Administration of this State, thy servant, the Governor, the Legislature, and all in authority over us. Bless the persons here assembled; diffuse Thy holy spirit among us, and help us to trust in Jesus Christ as our Saviour, and conduct us to eternal life. We ask it for our Redeemer's sake—Amen.

On motion of Hon. HENRY L. FISH, NATHANIEL SANDS, Esq., of the City of New-York, President of the Commercial Union, was unanimously chosen PRESIDENT of the Convention.

On motion, the Hon. ISRAEL T. HATCH, of Buffalo, and M. M. CALEB, Esq., of New-York, were appointed as a Committee to conduct Mr. SANDS to the chair.

On taking the chair Mr. SANDS, made the following address to the Convention.

SPEECH OF NATHANIEL SANDS, ESQ., OF NEW-YORK.

GENTLEMEN OF THE CONVENTION—You will please accept my thanks for the honor you have conferred upon me in selecting me your President on this occasion. We can scarcely over-estimate the importance of the work we have on hand, and which we have met here to do, and to which we must give our most serious deliberation and attention. I see assembled here representative men from all parts of the State—merchants, public men, and working men—men who I know are in earnest in desiring to carry out a solid, substantial, lasting reform of the great canal system of the State of New-York. [Applause.] It would be, gentlemen, singular after we have received from our forefathers these grand public works, if we had not intelligence, energy, and strength enough to take care of them. I see that some gentleman has laid upon the table the history of the origin of the Erie Canal; those who have perused this pamphlet can appreciate what this great public work was. When it was originated the great State of New-York was poor; we had just passed through a war, and many thought that war had not yet ended, and that we should provide and set apart our resources for the contingencies which might arise. It has been said here that I am the President of the Commercial

Union of the State of New-York; having mentioned my name in connection with the Organization, it may not be uninteresting for me to give a few words in regard to the Union. On the 19th day of October last, there assembled in the City of New-York, a Convention made up of representatives from the Boards of Trade through the State of New-York, and from the Chamber of Commerce, the Produce Exchange, and the Citizens' Association of New-York. They assembled in convention, and the result of their deliberation was the organization of the Commercial Union of the State of New-York—an organization that intends to remain permanent as long as there is any work left to be accomplished; [applause] and so long as canals exist in this State there will be work to do.

You may change your systems annually, and men may come forward pledged to carry out your views, but gentlemen, it is the experience of all governments that it requires those who have interests to protect to be on hand to protect such interests. Therefore, in the Commercial Union of the State of New York, which has already commenced work in earnest, we will find this protection. It has now its organizations in no less than forty different towns and cities of this State, and we intend there shall be no town, city, or village bordering on the canal, where it shall not be put in effective working order. That Commercial Union intends to have an Executive Committee in every town and city, and that Executive Committee is to take charge of particular sections of the canal, and see that the work is fairly, thoroughly and economically performed. The canals, and their condition throughout the whole State of New-York, to-day speak to you in far more eloquent language than any I can utter.

The subjects with which, I suppose, this Convention will consider itself called upon to deal, are first: The enactment of such laws as will give us an efficent system for the management of the canals, so as to increase the facilities of trade, and also to fix the responsibility upon the officials charged with the important duties in connection with them; we wish to fix the responsibility where it belongs; we do not want to go to an official and when we call him to account for what he has done, to have him turn around and say, "It is not to me you must come with such complaints; go to another officer." The second proposition is a thorough revision of the rates of toll, and their reduction to a point consistent with all the interests involved. The third is the introduction of steam, and of improved facilities for securing rapid and certain transportation. We want no delay. It may be rapid this week, or this month and delay next month. This is fatal to a successful management of the canal, and we want *rapidity, certainty, economy and efficiency.*

Sir Walter Raleigh said, many years ago, and it is as true to-day as when he said it, "Whosoever commands the sea commands the trade of the world; and whosoever commands the trade of the world, commands the riches of the world, and consequently the world itself;" and we can say with as much truth, that so long as we command the great water highway to the West, uniting the Atlantic Ocean with the father of waters flowing down the valley of the Mississippi, we command the trade of the West, with its vast resources, for our mutual and lasting benefit. We offer the great Western States what they so much demand, an open, and, I trust, in time, a free pathway to the sea; and we desire in return the vast benefit of carrying their products to market. You know the geographical position of our State is most favorable; resting on the Atlantic Ocean on the south it stretches out westward touching the great Lakes and opening up its arms to its Western sisters to welcome their products. It has been alleged, and perhaps with some truth, that one of our national characteristics is a disposition to self-glorification; but who can contemplate the history of our country, its resources and extent, and feel that it is not only not surpassed by any other, but is equaled by no other upon the planet. It is plainly manifest that He who is in all and over all and through all, and without whose notice not a single sparrow falls to the ground, has set apart a spot between the Atlantic and Pacific Oceans which embraces our favored land, a spot where the human race shall develop and flower out in all its strength and beauty.

In the olden time when boats passed down the Rhine it was customary for the petty barons to levy tribute on every vessel as it passed along, and when it reached the market to which it was destined scarcely any portion of its cargo was left. Now we do not wish to pursue this policy in relation to our Western sisters; we must extend the right hand of fellowship in earnest, and invite them to use this highway to the sea at so low a cost that they will regard our invitation as coming from men who mean them well. Come one, come all, you are welcome to all our uses, rights and privileges; you are heirs and joint heirs with us. The West, in its large and generous spirit, will respond to a sentiment like this, and a large share of her vast products will begin to flow down our canals to market.

The great canal system has fallen into dilapidation because the people have never organized to protect their rights. Having learned so severe a lesson in the past, they will act differently in the future, and they have organized, to defend their rights, the "COMMERCIAL UNION OF THE STATE OF NEW-YORK." I cannot better enforce the necessity of this movement than by quoting the language of that able legislative report on the "Present condition of the State Canals," made January 22d, 1868. That document declares: "The cry comes up from every quarter of the State that this evil must be remedied; the millions of property now going to waste, and which failed to reach its destined market, demand it; the consequent derangement of trade demands it; the fair fame of the State demands it. We may not turn a deaf ear to the appeal for succor."

There are those, and their number is not small, who say that a Republican form of Government is a failure, and they despair of even reaching good government, and of seeing the faithful administration of public trusts by men of large and comprehensive views and unblemished honor. But I am not among that number. I believe and know that we are working out not only our temporal but our eternal salvation under the great law of progress which is being carried on and developed in this land, and which will be carried on until we have the most perfect form of government in all its details, that ever existed on the face of this earth. [Applause.] Good Government, like every blessing, is the result of laborious and well directed effort, of constant and unceasing vigilance. Those men who founded this Government did their work well in their day and generation; we have traded too largely upon their capital, we have neglected many duties belonging to a sovereign people, and to-day we are reaping the fruits of that neglect. History teaches us how a single mind can impress itself upon the world and mould its destinies. The names of Columbus, Cæsar, Washington and Napoleon, are sufficient to illustrate this great truth. I am no hero worshipper. I believe that what solid workingmen have accomplished in the past, can be accomplished in the future. Each age has its mission, and each day has its duties—we have ours, and one among them is to inaugurate a new era in the management of the great canal system of the State of New-York.

Gentlemen of the Convention, let us see to it that our work is well done, and done quickly. I leave this work in your hands, and now await the further pleasure of this Convention.

On motion the following Vice-Presidents were chosen for the Convention:

ISRAEL T. HATCH,
MILLARD FILLMORE,
ALEXANDER BRUSH,
ASHER P. NICHOLS,
S. S. GUTHRIE,
NILES CASE,
HIRAM NILES,
G. S. HAZARD,
GEORGE W. TEFFT,
of Buffalo.

DAVID J. MITCHELL,
WILLIAM D. STEWART,
of Syracuse.

WILLIAM F. ALLEN,
O. H. HASTINGS,
M. MERICK,
W. W. WRIGHT,
W. H. HERRICK,
D. G. FORT,
of Oswego.

S. G. CHASE,
C. W. ARMSTRONG,
E. P. EASTON,
of Albany.

FRANK LAKEY,
of Palmyra.

M. M. CALEB,
L. J. N. STARK,
JESSE HOYT,
FRANCIS D. MOULTON,
EDWARD HINCKEN,
E. W. COLEMAN,
WILLIAM E. DODGE,
S. D. HARRISON,
DAVID DOWS,
J. M. FISKE,
RICHARD B. CONNOLLY,
CARLOS COBB,
E. S. BROWN,
E. A. TOMPKINS,
S. K. LANE,
B. P. BAKER.
A. H. PHILLIPS,
R. H. LAIMBEER,
GEORGE W. SMITH,
A. R. GRAY,
U. C. WHITLOCK,
F. J. WEEKS,
of New-York.

L. D. COLLINS,
of West Troy.

T. SCOTT LEDYARD,
of Wayne.

E. E. DAVIS,
E. MARTIN,
of Whitehall.

D. A. SHERMAN,
of Newark.

CHARLES STANFORD,
of Schenectady.

A. E. CULVER,
J. E B. THORNE,
R. H. KISSAM,
of Utica.

GEORGE C. BURDETT,
G. L. DOUGLAS,
P. A. MOORE,
of Troy.

EDWARD M. SMITH,
HENRY L. FISH,
JAMES M. WHITNEY,
GEORGE G. COOPER,
JOHN WILLIAMS,
GEORGE J. WHITNEY,
of Rochester.

DAVID UNDERWOOD,
of Fort Edward.

RICHARD CROWLEY,
of Lockport.

SILAS H. WITHERBEE,
of Port Henry.

ALLEN C. BEACH,
of Watertown.

On motion JOSEPH F. DALY, Esq., of the City of New-York, was chosen Secretary of the Convention.

W. LACY, W. P. ROBINSON, WILLIAM THURSTON, E. ANGEVINE, H. C. DANIELS, S. C. BENJAMIN and T. J. NEVILLE were on motion chosen to be Assistant Secretaries.

A delegation from the City of Toledo, Ohio, consisting of Messrs. C. A. KING, A. L. BACKUS, E. WILLIAMS, P. B. JOHNSON and D. B. SMITH, of Toledo, was then introduced by Mr. G. S. HAZARD, of Buffalo, who moved that they be invited to take part in this Convention. The motion was carried unanimously.

The President extended the invitation to the Toledo delegation.

On motion the following Committee was appointed to prepare business for the Convention:

HENRY L. FISH,
HENRY B. KNAPP,
of Rochester.

E. S. BROWN,
E. H. TOMPKINS,
E. W. COLEMAN,
of New-York.

CYRUS CLARK,
NILES CASE,
of Buffalo.

D. G. FORT,
of Oswego.

CHARLES NICHOLS,
JOHN J. CROUSE,
of Syracuse.

PERRY E. TOLES,
of Troy.

C. H. MALLORY,
of Utica.

E. A. MARTIN,
of Whitehall.

C. A. SWEET,
of Albany.

On motion the following Committee was appointed to draft and report Resolutions:

DAVID J. MITCHELL,
WM. D. STEWART,
of Syracuse.

A. S. JEWELL,
FRANCIS D. MOULTON,
of New-York.

C. P. EASTON,
of Albany.

E. E. DAVIS,
of Whitehall.

HIRAM NILES,
P. S. MARSH,
of Buffalo.

PHILIP J. MEYER,
G. H. PERKINS,
of Rochester.

A. E. CULVER,
of Utica.

L. D. COLLINS,
of West Troy.

The following Letters addressed to the Convention were then read by Mr. JOSEPH F. DALY, the Secretary.

LETTER OF HON. WILLIAM F. ALLEN.

STATE OF NEW-YORK,
COMPTROLLER'S OFFICE,
ALBANY, *Jan.* 15, 1870.

Nathaniel Sands, Esq., President of Commercial Union of the State of New-York:

SIR:—I have the honor to acknowledge an invitation to attend a Convention of the Commercial Union at Rochester, on the 19th instant, and regret that engagements that cannot be deferred will prevent my attendance. The subjects proposed to be considered are of great moment, and deeply interesting to the business community, and I have no doubt will receive at the hands of the Convention the deliberate and disinterested consideration to which they are entitled.

If the wisdom and experience of the Convention shall be able to devise a reformed system for the official management of the canals by which their efficiency and usefulness can be increased and their trade improved, the public will gratefully accept the results.

Whether the present repairing and superintending of the canal by contract, is among the subjects that will be considered, is not indicated by the note of invitation. But that question is now presented in the discussion of the subject of canal management. It is certainly worthy of consideration at this time, when very many are urging an abandonment of the system.

Yours respectfully,

WM. F. ALLEN.

LETTER OF Hon. RICHARD B. CONNOLLY.

CITY OF NEW-YORK,
Department of Finance,
Comptroller's Office,
January 14, 1870.

Gentlemen of the Commercial Union:

DEAR SIRS—I am in receipt of your invitation to attend a General Convention of the Commercial Union, to be held in the City of Rochester on the 19th inst., and in reply I have to say that I fully concur with your committee in the great importance which attaches to this subject, and of "reforming the official management and improving the trade of the canals of the State of New-York." While a member of the Senate of this State, I had abundant opportunities to learn from official sources the inestimable value of our canals to the internal trade and commercial importance, as well as the prosperity and grandeur of the State in all its material interests.

From the earliest history of the canals of this State there has been a difference of opinion as to the best means of making them the most available as a medium of communication through the State from the tide water, as well as between the important points of local traffic. And while these practical measures have required time and experience to adjust them to an economical standard, as a source of public revenue, the railroad element has grown to an importance in the line of competition that is well calculated to alarm the friends of the canals, as to the future administration of this important branch of our State policy.

In the recent annual message of Gov. Hoffman, the total abolition of the contract system is urged as essential to a more economical management of the canals.

I think this is a wise recommendation of the Governor, and I concur with him, and doubt not this measure, if adopted, would prove beneficial.

In my opinion the interests of the people, who are engaged in the trade and traffic on the canals, as well as the true policy of the State, would be promoted by a system which would make our canals an economical mode of transit for all descriptions of traffic, both foreign and domestic. The canals should be so managed as to deliver a barrel of flour or pork, and other produce, into the New-York market from Buffalo and the far West, at a rate lower than could be possibly done by the railroads. An economical administration of the canals would, it is believed, accomplish this reform, and I trust the Convention may, in its superior wisdom, inquire into this branch of the canal policy.

With great respect,
Your obedient servant,
RICHARD B. CONNOLLY.

Nathaniel Sands, President; Henry L. Fish, M. M. Caleb, Niles Case, Jeremiah P. Robinson, Edward Hincken, Cheney Ames, L. J. N. Stark, State Central Committee; Joseph F. Daly, Secretary.

LETTER OF PETER COOPER, Esq.

THE CITIZENS' ASSOCIATION OF NEW-YORK,
Rooms, 813 Broadway,
January 15, 1870.

The President and Members of the Commercial Union of the State of New-York:

GENTLEMEN—I have received your invitation to attend a general Convention of the Commercial Union, which is to be held at Rochester on January 19th, for the purpose of considering the best means of reforming the official management and improving the trade of the canals of the State of New-York.

I perceive with pleasure that the great subject—the improvement of the canal system—has awakened so much attention in all parts of our State, and has called into existence a powerful society—the "Commercial Union"—which extends through the whole canal region, and is organized on an indestructible basis.

I have for many years resided in New-York City, and have for a period, almost beyond the experience of any living men, been interested myself in the growth and prosperity of our city and our State, and of those great public works to which so much of that prosperity is due. I have seen the Erie Canal bring to our storehouses the wealth of the West, and the lateral canals opening up the resources of our own State. Long before the railroads increased traffic to its present proportions, the Erie Canal was building up this Commonwealth through its great facilities for freight, and even now with all the railroad competition this central water-way can be made to carry more freight and pay better than at any other period in its history. The Erie Canal must always be a necessity, so long as New-York City is a commercial centre, and I fully believe that a great part of the prosperity of the city depends upon the canal.

But to make these water-ways what they should be, demands wisdom in administration and watchful care on the part of the citizens of our State; and I see the greatest encouragement to the friends of the canals in the institution of this Commercial Union and the calling of this Convention. I trust and believe that your deliberations will be guided by sound discretion and wisdom, and that your voice, destined to be potent with the Legislative councils, will be raised to demand for the canals a good system, thorough repairs, cheap tolls, and increased speed in transportation. With these the Erie Canal will attract millions of dollars of trade now diverted from our State, and will increase the prosperity of the people.

With the heartiest wishes for your success, and the fullest confidence in the result of the Convention,

I remain,

Most truly yours,

PETER COOPER, *President.*

LETTER OF HON. ASHER P. NICHOLS.

BUFFALO, *January* 18, 1870.

GENTLEMEN—I have received your invitation to attend the Canal Convention at Rochester, on the 19th and 20th inst., for which I am greatly obliged. I had hoped to be there, but at the last find myself unavoidably deprived of that pleasure. So hearty, however, is my sympathy with your purpose of reforming the official management, and improving the trade of the canals of the State, that I must needs express it. Any effort looking to that result will always command my earnest co-operation. And the time, too, it seems to me, is propitious for organizing a thorough and efficient movement in their behalf. The public mind is fully informed, I cannot doubt, as to the many sore and grievous burthens under which our canal interests groan. They must be lifted off, or death will ensue, and that speedily. The crisis is upon us. Are the people equal to the emergency? I believe they are, and as one of the many evidences I hail gladly your Convention, and wish it God-speed in the good work. The prime and vital importance of our canals I assume; that need not be proved. In an honorable competition among equals, they have given us wealth, commercial ascendancy, fame. Not to our State alone; as mighty powers of civilization, they have opened, peopled, developed and enriched the great West and North west. Their decadence and death would not only be the index of our waning power and decrepitude, but would cover us with merited ignominy.

The true policy of a State is an enlightened self-interest. New-York wants the commerce and carrying trade tending to the Atlantic seaboard. She demands it, because she can give it the greatest facilities. Its track of transit is naturally through and over her territory, and it is the high duty of the State to foster and strengthen this advantage. Our rivalry with other States and routes is an open, an honorable one; let them do their best—we will do ours. With our canals properly managed and equipped, we can maintain and increase our present vantage ground. Is there any insuperable difficulty in this? Is there any magic about canals which makes them m›re difficult of management than other enterprises? Certainly not. The same fair measure of intelligence, care and integrity, sufficient for other interests, is sufficient here. What is wanted is the will and the purpose; all else will come readily enough. *Get the Canals out of the hands of interested men, back into the guardianship of the State, and the great difficulty is overcome; the rest is matter of detail.*

These interests are too vast and precious to be entrusted to interested discretion. Nothing but the higher guardianship of the State will suffice for this trust. As the first step in this direction, what is known as the "repair contract system" must be abolished—cut up by the roots. A bill for that purpose has already been introduced, I am happy to see, into the Senate. I trust it will speedily become a law. This system cannot, in my judgment, be successfully defended in any point of view. Few words need be wasted upon it. It contains within itself a fatal defect; it has a taint of original sin that no legislative grace can remove. It may be expressed almost in a single word—*it tends directly and inevitably to corrupt the men who have the contracts.* They are human, and can resist but about so much; beyond this they yield. It is the first dictate of common sense, then, to remove this temptation. How can the contractor be expected to come up to the full measure of good navigable repair—which rests in opinion—when his profits are lessened by the amount of every dollar he expends for what *cupidity* suggests may be left undone? You have no right to expect it; it is not in human nature. This letting out at discretion to the lowest bidder, is the application of the competitive principle to a subject matter to which, in the nature of things, it is inapplicable, and it must be abandoned, as alike pernicious in theory and practice. That the canals under the guardianship of the State, and with the ordinary share of intelligence, care and honesty, may be thoroughly and economically managed, is a proposition as clear to my mind as that any other business, with the same elements, can be prosperously conducted. There is no intrinsic difficulty in the case. It is a simple question of capacity and honesty. The State has managed them well once, and can do so again. I utterly discard and repudiate the idea that the State is unequal to this great trust. There is some public virtue left yet. There are honest and capable public servants yet to be found. The errors of the past will serve as warnings for the future. I repeat, the State is equal to this great trust. The doubling the single locks is under contract. These completed, and the canals given the full capacity of their legal dimensions, and kept on a footing of efficiency and equipment equal to such capacity, and I have no fears that they will, for years, answer all demands upon them, and do their full share towards the maintenance and increase of our commercial position. They are not now in a condition to do what their legal capacity will permit, and we have no more right to expect it than we should have to look for full speed in a horse with a crippled leg. Other improvements will follow. That steam, in some form, will soon take its place on the canals, as a propelling power, I have no doubt. The enterprise of our people will compel it, and genius will find a way. The toll-sheet must be revised, and tribute to the State, for the use of its canals, be reduced to the lowest point practicable, with reference to our other obligations. The great compensation must be found, hereafter, in diffused benefits among the people. Free and unfettered commerce, so to speak, is the pressing demand of the time. The cry must be heeded. Old exactions, proper at the time, must give way, charges be lightened, and new facilities granted. Where these inducements are found, in largest measure, there, other things being equal, the greatest volume of commerce will flow, and, like the Nile, enrich every interest along its course. We know that we have the best natural route, and we ought to realize that nothing but our own criminal indifference can ever deprive us of its advantage.

But some say that the era of canals is past, and that railroads are now the order of the day. I do not think so. On the contrary I believe there is no hurtful antagonism between them, and that with increasing needs there is ample room for both, each performing the service best adapted to it. Let it be borne in mind that the objective point in all this matter, for which we strive, is the maintenance and growth of the present commercial ascendancy of New-York, as the great carrier to the seaboard; and then all the canals ask is fair play. They ask no discrimination against railroads, but they do demand what of right belongs to them—restoration to their full capacity, ample facilities, and honest and capable management. True they are no longer the exclusive channels of commerce they once were, but they are none the less useful. Nay, they have an added function now, as regulators of freights, made necessary by the railroads. These, it will be remembered are private enterprises, urged on by all the eagerness and zeal of individual interest, while the canals, freed from this pressure of private gain, exercise a kind of State function through the operation of the laws of trade, protecting the people against the over-exactions and oppressions, inevitaby resulting from the unchecked sway of personal interests.

But I must stop. What was intended as the expression of sympathy with the object of your Convention has, almost of itself, run into a hurriedly-written letter, and yet not the half, or tithe of half, is said. Many topics of the highest moment in this connection, as the financial questions, rival routes, &c., &c., I leave untouched. I beg you to excuse my troubling you with so much. My only apology is the paramount interest I take in the subject matter you have in hand. I fervently hope a brighter day is about to dawn on our canals. I know the earnest and patriotic purpose of the promoters of the convention, and I also recognize their practical good sense and great sagacity.

From such a Convention, in such a cause, I cannot but hope for most beneficial results.

     I am, gentlemen,
      Yours respectfully,

         ASHER P. NICHOLS.

HENRY L. FISH,   EDWARD HINCKEN,
M. M. CALEB,   CHENEY AMES,
NILES CASE,   L. J. N. STARK,
JEREMIAH P. ROBINSON,
    State Central Committee of the Commercial Union.

    NATHANIEL SANDS, *President.*
JOSEPH F. DALY, *Secretary.*

LETTER OF HON. WILLIAM E. DODGE.

CHAMBER OF COMMERCE OF THE STATE OF
NEW-YORK, INSTITUTED A. D. 1768.
NEW-YORK, *January* 15*th*, 1870.

President and Members of the Commercial Union of the State of New-York:

GENTLEMEN—The commercial interests of the City of New-York are so intimately connected with the preservation of the State Canals, that every movement for the improvement of their management and trade must enlist the warmest sympathies and support of our citizens.

The cheapest freight route is undoubtedly a well managed canal, and with the aid of the great central water-way, the Erie Canal, this State and this City can command the trade of the West without the possibility of competition.

But it requires extraordinary vigilance and wisdom in the face of modern competition, to keep the canals popular with freighters and with the people. The canals, to hold their own, and engross the mass of traffic for which they were intended, must preserve eminently these distinctive features:

1. They must be managed by officials who desire to see them prosper.
2. They must be so cheap as to tolls, as to defy competition.
3. They must by every possible means be made as rapid a means of transit as modern scientific inventions can effect.
4. They must be made popular with the people at large by economical management and the adoption of a system of repairs, which is sure to keep them in good order at a fair cost.

The objects of the Commercial Union, which are to watch over these great works with unceasing vigilance, to protect them from the corruption which too often taints official administration, and to preserve them for the good of our State and our City, are worthy in the highest degree of support. The convention of such a body to consider this great subject cannot but be harmonious and successful in action, and I feel confident that your deliberations will result in the greatest benefit to the cause you have in hand.

I regret that important business in connection with the Indian Commission will require me to be in Washington at the time your Convention is to be held. Having been for thirty years connected with our Railroad system, and for twelve years a Director in the Erie, when it was an honor to be such, I have always contended the prosperity of our roads leading West would be best promoted by the enlargement of our canal, so that the coarse products of the soil could be shipped from the Far West to the seaboard, at a profit to the producers, giving them the ability to purchase freely such goods as would pay to be transported by rail, and give them the means to visit the East often, thus furnishing the roads with their most valuable business—passengers. I have always contended that our wheat, corn, barley and oats should have a cheap water communication, and hope the day will come when our canal will be doubled in size and the boats propelled by steam. This is what New-York and the West needs.

With my best wishes for the success of the Convention,

I am, very respectfully, yours,

W. E. DODGE,
President of the New-York Chamber of Commerce.

LETTER OF Hon. THOMAS PARSONS.

ROCHESTER, *Jan.* 19, 1870.

Mr. President and Gentlemen of the Convention:

It is a matter of sincere regret to me that, through sickness, I am deprived of the pleasure of meeting with you in Convention to-day. I have ever been a warm friend of the Erie Canal, and whenever anything could be done to promote its interests, increase its traffic, or reduce the cost of transportation thereon, I have ever been ready, laying politics aside, to respond to the calls made upon me. This principle, I trust, will be adopted by the Convention now in session; for to produce necessary reforms, it will require unity of action regardless of politics. That there is need of reform and reorganization in the management of the public works, no person at all conversant with their present condition and prospects can question; and such changes in their management should be made, to command a sure, quicker and cheaper mode of transit.

The question arises: What can be done, and how shall we obtain the desired result? I hesitate not a moment in replying that I would do justice to the present repair contractors, and at once abolish the repair contract system, adopting the State repair system, with direct responsibility on the part of the State Engineer and Canal Commissioners, with proper restrictions and guards to protect the public interest.

I would also immediately reduce the tolls to one-half the present rates, on every article now transported on the canals, and on those articles not now carried at all, or to any material extent, I would abolish the tolls entirely.

I would cause to be put in permanent repair immediately the long level at Utica, and also the long level from Rochester to Lockport, and the Canal from Lockport to Buffalo, by bottoming out the same to its full requirements, and solidly repair the stone walls, so as to withstand the wash of steam-towing; for I believe steam-power, in connection with horse-power, on the short levels, could be successfully used, and materially expedite the passage of boats to and from tide water, for it would give, out of say 350 miles of canal navigation, 153 miles applicable for steam. The great object sought for is to cheapen the cost of transportation, " with a reduction of tolls as proposed;" " shortening the time of transit," and " keep the canal in perfect order." This object would be obtained, so far as it is possible, with the present size of the Erie Canal; but, Mr. President, you and the gentlemen composing this Convention may rest assured that unless the great and final enlargement be speedily pushed forward, the amount of tonnage now annually transported will gradually be reduced, so that the canal, instead of being the regulator of freights, will only become the dependant for the crumbs that may fall from their master's table. I will here cite one fact, which will bear me out in the assertion just made. In the year 1862 there was transported on the canals the products of agriculture, 2,152,159 tons, while from the same source in the year 1868 only 1,229,544 tons were transported; and, if I am correctly informed, the year 1869 was even less than 1868, making a decrease of over 1,000,000 tons. I do not deny but that a portion of the loss may be temporarily regained, but it cannot be permanently retained until the final enlargement is accomplished. It is asserted by those unfriendly to the canals, that the days of water-carriage are among the past; but it is not true, witness the commerce on the Lakes. What the Lakes are, so far as water-carriage, the Erie Canal by enlargement can be made to be. Wheat and other grain in proportion to it, during the season of navigation, is freighted from the Upper Lake ports to Buffalo, at an average cost not exceeding 9 cents per bushel. The Erie Canal, by an enlargement thereof worthy of the Empire State, will do it for the same sum. Then will not the great commercial interest of this State prove equal to the emergency pending before them, and with their teeming millions of property cause the canal to be enlarged to a capacity putting it beyond the peradventure of failure hereafter?

It is claimed on the part of the Western producer that wheat cannot be raised profitably at a sum less than one dollar per bushel. It has only brought the producer the past year from sixty to seventy cents per bushel. The consumers in the Eastern States complain that while wheat is only worth seventy cents where it is raised, they are obliged to pay $1.50 per bushel, and that the difference of eighty cents per bushel for freight, &c., is an extortion put upon them by those handling the article between the producer and consumer.

Mr. President, the great object of the Convention is to devise ways and means to do the best that can possibly be done with the canals as you find them, and for the purpose of expediting and lessening the cost of transportation as compared with the past; and I have no doubt that satisfactory conclusions as to what is best will be arrived at, by the intelligent and experienced gentlemen composing the Convention.

In conclusion, I would simply refer to the past by stating that the first cargo of grain received from the Upper Lakes, at Buffalo, was from Grand Haven, Michigan, in the year 1836, about 11 years after the Erie Canal was completed, and only 34 years ago. We have, therefore, cause for rejoicing when we consider what the Erie Canal has done and is still doing for the Great West. In 1866 the arrival and departure from Buffalo was upwards of 14,000 vessels; what the number was in 1869 I know not; perhaps some gentleman from Buffalo can inform the Convention.

I am, with great respect,

THOMAS PARSONS.

The Hon. HORATIO SEYMOUR was then introduced by the President to the Convention, and was received with prolonged applause.

SPEECH OF Hon. HORATIO SEYMOUR.

Gentlemen of the Convention:

I owe this invitation to address you to the fact that during my life I have had occasion to know much of the history of the canals. For many years I was Chairman of the Canal Committee in the Legislature of this State—nay, more than that, from my earliest infancy I was connected with those who had to do with the origin and construction of the Erie Canal; and, living upon the banks of this great work, I have had every opportunity of seeing much of its management.

In giving you my views to-day, I am happy to say, at the outset, that I shall have no occasion to reflect upon the policy or conduct of party or of men. (Applause.) The mistakes into which we have fallen have been, in some degree, the result of circumstances, and we are now called upon to correct evils which had their origin in good intention.

Our canals, at this time, are laboring under a cloud of public misapprehension that has grown out of many circumstances. In the first place, many men think because railroads have been brought into use after canals, that they, in a great degree, supercede them. There can be no greater mistake than this. You need your railroads to carry the population into different parts of your country, and after they have once taken possession of the soil, you need water transportation to carry their products to market. (Applause.) No community can be prosperous where the cheap, coarse, common productions of the country have no value, or there is not a ready and cheap mode of transporting them to where they are needed and will have value. This question of transportation is the great question of the day. It underlies the whole of the financial problem, and unless it has a proper solution our finances cannot be put in a proper condition. It is said that property is a thing in the right place, and unless it is in the right place it is no property,—a stone that obstructs the field where the farmer ploughs the soil is valuable property in the city where it is needed. Gold, which we value so highly, when it is fast in the mine where it will cost more than it is worth to bring it forth, is of no value. We find thus that all our wisest statesmanship resolves itself into this question of putting things into the right places. To-day a bushel of wheat sells on the prairies of Iowa for forty cents. The low price causes distress. There would be no such distress if it was not that the cost of transportation of the staple products is so great that they cannot be carried to the markets of the East or the markets of Europe. If we had an outlet that would enable us to place the valuable productions of our country, at a small cost, where they are needed, we would have no trouble about the public debt, taxation and questions of that nature.

When property bears a high value and represents a large sum, the interest on that sum is also augmented, and he who owns it seeks speed in its transportation. When wheat was worth more than two dollars per bushel West, the man who had two dollars invested in a bushel, hurried it to the market. The cost of its transportation was a small percentage on that sum. For this reason the whole carrying trade of our country during the last two years has been in an unnatural condition. It has been forced on railroads beyond what the ordinary laws of trade and commerce would direct. But if the value of a bushel of wheat in Iowa is forty cents, and in Wisconsin it is sixty or sixty-five cents, the man who buys wheat does not inquire how quick he can get it to market, but how cheaply he can place it there. A charge which was ten per cent. on the price of wheat a year ago, is twenty per cent. on its value now. We see then, at once, that a vast amount of business has been forced on the railroads, by high prices, which does not belong there. I congratulate those who are engaged in business on our canals, that we have now reached a crisis in our affairs, and the public will be taught that canals are essential to the business and prosperity of our country. (Applause.)

What are we to do in view of the fact that we are to expect a large increase of business on the canal? The question comes up, what are our present duties? I wish to confine my remarks to one single consideration—what can we do to make the business of our canals prosperous in this year of 1870? What can we do to replenish the pockets of those who have lost money during the last two or three years, and who have also lost somewhat of their courage in carrying on this branch of industry?

The first difficulty you will meet in the coming spring is, that you will find your canal choked up with mud, and choked up with tolls. At one time when we had dug out three feet of earth we actually put in four feet of toll. Now, it does not matter to the carrier whether his boat drags on the bottom or drags on the toll. There has been with our public men a great misapprehension as to the public feeling on this subject; they say if you reduce the tolls you will immediately alarm the business men of the country and the farmers of the country. Now, I am a farmer; not a skillful one, but one living on a farm, and have looked carefully into what concerns its interests. The farmers of the State, with the exception of Western New-York men, are the consumers and not the producers of breadstuffs, and when you reach the western boundaries of the State you find they want low tolls. It is a mistaken view that men take, when they look upon these canals as instruments simply to make money. It was not in that spirit they were built, and not in that spirit they are now to be considered by any man who is able to take enlarged views of the interest of our State, and of the interest of our country. While I do not ask that we shall go to the length of abolishing our tolls altogether, while I do not believe it would be expedient to do that, I do not hesitate to say that we never raised one dollar of toll that did not cost us ten in the injury done to industry and commerce. What is the advantage this Erie Canal gives to us? What is the advantage to taxpayers and farmers? It is this,—that it has built up along its line great manufacturing towns which pay taxes and lighten the load of the rural districts; it has made a home market where the farmer can sell his coarse productions; it has made New-York the great commercial State of the country, giving employment to mechanics, and giving life to manufacture. What is all the toll we get from the Erie Canal compared with this? giving wealth to our State, and more than that giving strength to our Union,—because it unites each State together in the strong bonds of commerce. (Applause.)

If our canals were destroyed, increased railroad charges would crush out industry. The weight of State and National Debt and interest would be let down upon land, for commerce and manufacture would wilt.

There are no acts of government which call for more thought and skill than the levying of taxes. The scales of commerce are so nicely balanced that they are turned by the slightest weight. Three cents is a trivial sum; but it will turn the point whether a bushel of wheat shall or shall not be bought in the Western States. If it shall waste in the granaries or give life to commerce, it is a question which a small profit or loss will decide. To-day it may be worth but fifty cents in the hands of the farmers. If it goes to Europe—when it reaches there, it becomes worth three times as much. If it does not go to market, the business of the country loses not only the price the farmer should get, but also twice as much more, which would have been paid to the merchant and carriers and other classes. An unwise tax of three cents may cost the country one hundred and fifty cents. More than this, our commerce loses the return trade, which we should get from Europe, which makes the whole loss more than two dollars. The people of this State lose nearly half of this sum. A slight cutting down of tolls would give to the citizens of New-York more than all the revenues we get from our canals, not by the saving of taxes on the canals alone, but by the lower charges made in consequence by railroads and the profits thus given to industry. It is one of the strange objections sometimes made by officials, that if tolls were lowered the railroads would also put down their freights, so that the canal business would not be increased. In other words, that the people in every part of the country, and along all routes, would be helped every time taxation upon canal commerce is lightened. Well meaning public officers, who see but little of trade and industry, fall into the mistake of looking upon our canals as mere instruments of taxation, which are most valuable when they tax the highest and extort the largest sums.

As to the condition of our public works, the great difficulty the canals are laboring under, is the fact that the power has been misplaced. I repeat it, the power of the canals has been misplaced. When the Erie Canal was built it was at a time when Western New-York was a wilderness; it was made by men without experience, and we were obliged to send to Europe for a man to show us how to make a lock. This canal was built through a wilderness, through unhealthy swamps, by men without experience, without a knowledge of the work or of the materials they were to use; with all these difficulties they built a canal that cost about $6,000,000; the Erie and Champlain Canals together cost about $7,000,000.

How was it that we were able to build canals then, under those adverse circumstances, while to-day we all seem to fail so lamentably? The Erie Canal was a work carried on by men who had power to say what should be done; in the next place, through an intimate acquaintance with the work, they became interested in this matter—there was a sympathy felt for the canal; they appreciated the importance of the enterprise—every contractor felt his responsibility. I can remember the day when a contractor of the State of New-York felt that he was a public official, proud of doing his work well. Why? Because when a man performed his work well he got credit for it; it was well done; he was a man trusted by the officials of the State, and when he met an official of the State he felt as a man should feel, helping to make a great public work; and every boatman found in the public official a man who sympathized with him. There was once an identification between the State and those who navigated our canals, and it is to that circumstance that we owe a vast deal of our former successes. When you give the power and control of the expenses of any great work to a man who sits in his office and only sees the enormous amount of outlay, who sees nothing but the expenditures, it cannot be carried on with success, because in his mind all sympathy with the work will die out. It is a high merit in an officer if he looks with anxious scrutiny into every expenditure made by everybody else; but he must not be the man to dictate what shall or shall not be done.

One day after another you find that the power and control is passing out of the hands of your Commissioners. The Canal Commissioners are the men elected for the purpose of having less to say about the canals than any other three persons. (Laughter.) When you go to Albany, before the financial officers of the State, you are not always cheered by a look of sympathy, but feel the distrust with which men look at you. Now that would not be the case if the officer was familiar with the details, and under-·stood the subject you laid before him, and could see when you come before him that you were seeking the public good. You must give to the Canal Commissioner full power; and when he sees a thing wrong, he shall be authorized to make it right. If the man is unfit for his position, turn him out. Give him responsibility, and with responsibility you will have better officers. Lift up the office, give it new power, make him responsible for the condition of your works; and, if you don't do that, I do not care what system you may adopt, it will fail. Unless the Commissioners have power to act, and shall be encouraged to act by a public sentiment that will hold them responsible, you will never have a canal fit for navigation. You must have sympathy existing between your State and the canals. The State must look upon the boatmen as its partners. New-York furnishes the right of way, and the carriers the boats. They are partners, and they must look upon each other as such. Give the Commissioners full power, and place the canals under their direction and control in everything. But there is another thing wanted on the canal, in consequence of this misplaced power. What would be thought of the government of the City of New-York, if they should have no police system, and would allow one omnibus driver to tie his horses to the lamp-post, and another to drive heedlessly through the crowded street, endangering life and property? Yet a similar state of things exists on the canal. Law is almost unknown. Men who have their property on the canal, have not their property protected by a police system on that canal. I gave out at one time more than three hundred commissions to the Erie Railroad, under a law of the State of New-York, which authorized the Railroad Company to make their employés police officers; and I gave out a number of similar commissions to the Central Railroad. Now, this lawlessness has grown up because you have removed the power from those familiar with the canals, and given it to those who are not familiar with those great evils. An efficient police system would not cost one dollar, as there are officials enough to do the duty. It would save the State vast sums of money. It has been said, and truly, too, that we need speed on the canals. I suggest a method by which we can increase the speed. A forwarder told me, this morning, that boats ought to go in eight days from Albany to Buffalo, but they do not get through in twelve days. I asked him how much of that delay was caused by the little detentions, the little disorders that we can hardly name, which obstruct the passage of the canal; how these compared with the whole time that was lost, and he agreed with the opinion of many others who have looked into the subject, that there was not as much time lost by breaks and serious delays as from these small disorders, and the want of a proper and well regulated police system. Boats lose one-third of their time, because you have not the power lodged in the proper hands. If a worthless captain lays up his boat for the night, or grounds it, thereby causing unnecessary delay, there should be a power to take that man and lock him up. (Applause.) Let him feel that there is an efficient force of police over him to punish him when he does wrong, and to protect him when he does right, and in a little while you will improve the morals along the canal, as well as obtain an increase of speed. I firmly believe there is no measure you can adopt that will meet the wants of commerce as well as the measure that will place the power of governing the canal where it belongs, and such a measure will restore that sympathy that was once felt between the public officers and the men that navigate the canal.

I would give your Canal Board a power over these Canal Commissioners; not a power to say what they shall or what they shall not do; not a power to say what they shall or shall not expend, but a power to bring each man to account; and if they find an unfaithful officer, give them power to remove him. What they want is to feel that they have the strong arm of the State behind them, to help and encourage them in the prosecution of their duty, and enabling them to check and punish licentiousness and wrong.

We seek these reforms for the public good, and for the advancement and prosperity of the whole country. When we have wise legislation, that legislation helps to forward the interests of commerce, and will also promote the moral well-being of those engaged in the great artery of commerce. (Applause.)

The Convention then took a recess until half-past two o'clock, to await the Report of the COMMITTEE ON BUSINESS and the COMMITTEE ON RESOLUTIONS.

Upon re-assembling at half-past two o'clock, and being called to order, the Convention received the Reports of Committees.

Hon. HENRY L. FISH, Chairman of the Committee on Business, presented the following

REPORT UPON BUSINESS FOR THE CONVENTION.

First—The abolition of the contract system for repairing the canals; the repeal of the Act creating it, and the abrogation of all existing contracts.

Second—The vesting of power in Canal Boards to proceed and put the canals in thorough and efficient repair and to keep them so.

Third—That the Canal Commissioners, who are the executive officers of the Board, be allowed to appoint all necessary subordinates for performing their duty, and that each Commissioner be held personally responsible for the work on his division to the Canal Board.

Fourth—The reduction of tolls by the Canal Board and Legislature so as to attract freights, which have been diverted from the canals by high tolls and delays.

Fifth--The State Central Committee of this Commercial Union to take measures to introduce and urge the passage of a bill or bills to effect the improvements and obtain the benefits above enumerated.

Sixth—Funding the present canal debt, to extend over a period of eighteen years to enable a reduction of canal tolls.

On motion this Report was unanimously adopted.

Hon. DAVID J. MITCHELL, Chairman of the Committee on Resolutions, then presented the following Report of Resolutions, which were read by Mr. FRANCIS D. MOULTON to the Convention:

RESOLUTIONS REPORTED BY THE COMMITTEE.

WHEREAS, The prosperity, wealth and importance of the State of New-York are mainly due to its canals and the wisdom which projected them; and the necessity for these great water ways to transport the commerce of the West and develop the resources of our own State was never greater than at the present time. And owing to official mismanagement and dishonesty under the contract system, by which the canals have sunk under the contract system, by which the canals have sunk almost to decay, and owing to the unwise adoption of high tolls by which trade is diverted from the canals and State, these great public works are falling into disrepute, and becoming inefficient, unsafe, expensive and ruinous instead of becoming every year more useful, convenient, flourishing and popular; and

WHEREAS, This Convention called by the Commercial Union, and composed of all those persons in every section of the State engaged in commerce, directly or indirectly associated with the canals, is assembled to consider the foregoing matters, and to proclaim the feeling of the people regarding the misgovernment, errors and corruption which threaten the existence of our canals, to suggest a remedy for existing evils, and to ask for speedy relief. Therefore, be it

Resolved, That this Convention is of the unanimous opinion that upon the preservation of our canals, and the increase of their trade, depends the future prosperity of our State.

Resolved, That the present system of repairing the canals, by contract, is wholly inefficient and grossly corrupt, and that such contract system and the laws creating it and the outstanding contracts under it must be abolished if the canals and their trade are to be preserved.

Resolved, That the canal tolls upon such freight as is competed for by other routes of transportation must be reduced to a rate that will make such competition impossible, and will secure all such freight to our State canals.

Resolved, That the necessary improvements to the canals would lead naturally and without loss to any interests to improvements in the system of canal navigation.

Resolved, That the canals must be kept at all times needful in such condition as shall insure certainty, and safety, and speed in transportation, and that such official and legislative action should be had as would cheapen such transportation and increase the trade of the canals to their fullest capacity.

Resolved, That the State Central Committee of the Commercial Union be, and they are hereby requested and authorized, to prepare and present to the Legislature immediately, a bill framed so as to secure the benefits and improvements above enumerated, and that such committee on behalf of this Union and this Convention, and of the people and canal interests throughout the State herein represented, urge the passage of such bill or bills and take all active measures in relation thereto, and to secure the preservation and improvement of the canals.

Resolved, That inasmuch as the demands of the present Constitution require the payment of the canal debt within the next six years, we believe that the best interests of the State require that the said debt be funded to extend over a period of not less than eighteen years, in order that the toll sheet may be reduced to a point which will retain the business which, under the present excessive toll sheet, is being forced into other channels.

Upon the question of the adoption of the resolutions, the following addresses were made to the Convention:

SPEECH OF HON. ISRAEL T. HATCH.

Hon. ISRAEL T. HATCH, of Buffalo, in rising to second a motion to adopt the resolutions, said, in substance:

REMARKS BY MR. HATCH.

Conventions, year after year, have urged reduction of tolls, and a speedier and cheaper transportation. We propose now to take them at their word, and to inaugurate the policy of making the canals free. If the Constitution leaves the matter in doubt, we will take the doubt in our favor. The idea of free water-routes is not a new one. Louis the XIVth brought it into existence when the canal of Languedoc was completed. He granted the tolls to the engineer Reque, but they were no more than sufficient to keep the canal in repair. The idea of the Emperor was not one of benevolence to his people; but, with a single eye to the augmentation of his own revenues, he adopted the policy of taxing wealth already accumulated, instead of property actually in the course of transit or exchange. It is an interesting fact, that notwithstanding all the intervening vicissitudes and confiscations, the canal of Languedoc is in the hands of the Reque family at the present day.

We have been surging along under the Constitution of 1846 since that instrument was enacted. It seems that we can't get out of the rut of the Constitution made over twenty years ago. That Constitution prevents any adequate reduction of tolls on the canals.

You all know that we have lately had a Constitutional Convention. I take no credit to myself that I was a member of it. It was generally remarked throughout the State that it would never end; but it did end, and as soon as the people got hold of the Constitution which it produced, they ended the material work of it, and even laid the ghost of it. Notwithstanding all the great commercial changes of this modern era, this Convention recognized no necessity for any material change in the financial article, No. 7, of the hide-bound Constitution of 1846.

There is a class of men who still hold to the Constitution of 1846. It seems impossible for them to appreciate the important changes that have since taken place. They seem to me worse than old Rip Van Winkle, who slept through the Revolutionary War. He woke up after twenty years, and could then see that changes had taken place. Not so with these people. They seem determined to oppose the true condition and urgency of the age. These men are the "Old Mortalities" of our State, who live only in the memories of the past, and, with their chisels and mallets, renew its works, especially those of their own creation, oblivious of the progress of the times, and neglectful of their duties and requirements. Had their great master, the teacher of their financial philosophy, lived to the present day, he could not have failed to comprehend the situation, and to modify in accordance with the demands of the times, his own work which was intended for the population and commerce of twenty years ago, as his disciples are either unwilling to see or incapable of comprehending.

Instead of increasing the capacity of the canal in proportion to the business which would naturally arise from the transit of the rapidly increasing productions of the West, it has been and is so egregiously mismanaged, under the present notion of making repairs imperfectly, when they are made, and frequently of avoiding them when they ought to be made, that it has gradually become more shallow from the caving in of the bench walls; and State Engineer Richmond deemed it his duty to warn the State of New-York, in his last Annual Report, that "there is less capacity now than there was in 1849, and double the business to perform."

Mr. Hatch entirely agreed with the distinguished gentlemen who had preceded him, that the removal of the tolls is as important as the removal of the mud. The removal of the mud only permits boats to pass over the canal; that of the tolls attracts traffic to it; while high tolls will in the end entirely repel it. Therefore, no canal policy can be practical or statesmanlike which does not include the removal of both obstructions.

By the neglect of the great thoroughfare, the commerce of the West is being expelled from the State. An immense diversion of the grain trade has already taken place. Of the grain received at the ports of the Lakes on its way to the East, nearly 69,000,000 bushels were sent to other places than the commercial metropolis. Some portion of this grain was used for home consumption, but a considerable increase has taken place at other sea-ports on the Atlantic, while that at New-York has diminished. It is estimated that the productions of the West immensely exceed those of ten years ago, but within that period there has been no increase in the business of the canals.

By a supine and fatuous policy a large share of the trade that naturally would come through our own State is driven into the hands of active foreign neighbors, who are on the alert to receive it. The receipts of wheat and flour at Montreal alone last year were equivalent to nearly seven millions of bushels more than in the previous year.

Since the union of the Upper and Lower Provinces, and previous to 1867, Canada expended upon the rival route of the St. Lawrence nearly $6,000,000. We are now threatened with expenditures, in comparison with which those already made are trifling, and are left in no doubt as to their object. The Canadian Commissioner of Public Works asserts in his Report of 1867, printed by order of the House of Commons, that "those who designed the public works of Canada, besides desiring to provide for the immediate wants of the country, had also in view the prospects of the Western trade, and carried out their plans on such a scale as, in their estimation, would be commensurate with its requirements." While they are thus alive to the magnitude of the prize for which they contend with us, we unwisely rest on the merits of past success and of natural superiority already proved, heedless that in these days of strenuous competition, the ultimate victory can only belong to those who are vigilant and persevering in availing themselves to the fullest extent of the best facilities within their reach.

While the efforts thus described are made on the most northerly of the forwarding routes on this continent, we must not omit consideration also of the various lines erecting within the territory of this nation and competing with those of our own State. Our country is rapidly becoming a network of railroads, and some of them drain and cut off the grain trade on its way to the East without permitting it to touch Chicago.

Southward we find that active exertions have been made to turn the course of the grain trade down the Mississippi. Elevators have been erected at St. Louis and New Orleans, thus adding the facilities of transhipment and ventilation of the grain to that of cheap transit down the stream of that noble river. In this way grain may be carried from St. Louis to Liverpool, with only one transhipment, and that one is now economically effected by the best appliances of modern mechanical skill for that purpose. At all points where commerce to a sufficient extent is attracted on the great rivers of the West, elevators similar to those of St. Louis may be erected. There is little doubt that this will be done, and then, unless we cheapen the cost of transportation, many of the streams of trade which have made this State and our commercial greatness what they are, will be tapped and turned away from us.

Mr. Hatch stated that a plan was proposed to fund the debt for a period of eighteen years. It was approved and recommended by the Produce Exchange of New-York, and subsequently brought by him, last winter, before the State Legislature, where, although not presented until the session had almost closed, it came very near adoption, 59 votes being recorded in his favor and only 53 adversely.

The plan of funding public debt was introduced in England by Mr. Pitt, at whose name it was said the venal classes trembled in every portion of the Empire, and its results are such as to have conferred lasting honor upon his name. Our own general government is now endeavoring to apply the same principle in funding the national debt. Men of all political parties concur as to the soundness of this policy in regard to national affairs. Thus, in its application to the canal debt of the State, Mr. Hatch recommended the adoption of no new or merely experimental theory, but of a principle well tried, and sanctioned by the highest precedents, including even that section of the Constitution of 1846, under which he proposed to inaugurate the policy of a freeer and free canal.

He stated that the total canal debt of the State is now $12,564,780, less $3,213,021 in the Sinking Fund, leaving $9,351,759, to which is to be added the balance of the general fund debt, making the total over $12,000,000, for payment of which the canal revenues are sacredly pledged—while to create a new debt is expressly forbidden by the Constitution, except by an Act of the Legislature, subsequently approved by the people at a general election. Even then the law must also provide that a direct annual tax shall be collected to pay the interest on such debt as it falls due, and to discharge the principal within eighteen years after the creation of the debt. An amendment adopted in 1854 further provided that "the tolls on the canal should not be reduced below those of 1852, except by the Canal Board, with the concurrence of the Legislature." The effect of these various restrictions has been not only to prevent the State from meeting exigencies by improving the canal, but also from reducing tolls, even when this has been rendered absolutely necessary by rival routes both at home and abroad.

Mr. Hatch stated that the chief provisions of the plan proposed are: To pass a law conferring upon the Canal Board the power to readjust the toll—according to the necessities of the times—as fully and effectually as a board of railway directors has the power to adjust the freight tariff of the road under its control, thus enabling the trade of our State to compete on just and liberal terms with whatever rivalry may arise. As a considerable decrease of tolls might reduce the income from the canal below the amount required to fulfil the annual requirements of the Constitution of 1846, and the exaction of a direct tax might prove temporarily injurious to the political interests to which the Board might be friendly, Mr. H. proposed to remove the obstacles permanently out of the way, by authorizing the Commissioners of the Canal Fund to borrow an amount sufficient to fund the debt at eighteen years, the interest to be paid by direct tax, but only in case the surplus canal tolls should be insufficient for that purpose. He had high legal authority for asserting that such an Act would be entirely harmonious with the existing Constitution. When passed by the Legislature, it would be submitted to the people next November, and, if ratified, would then become operative. He contrasted the early benefits of such a law with the tedious and injurious delays that must arise from looking solely to the aid of a constitutional amendment, which could not be completed in less than three years.

A careful computation, made in the office of the Canal Auditor at Albany, demonstrates that an annual contribution of $338,635.54, invested at five per cent., will extinguish a debt of $10,000,000 in eighteen years. Allow $600,000 more for annual interest on the debt, and the whole sum needed yearly would be less than a million of dollars—not so much as one-third of the average net receipts from canal tolls during the last two years, the amounts having, even under the injudicious and unnecessarily expensive system of management, been $2,882,772.60 in 1869, and the previous year they were $3,293,301.13.

Thus, at one-third of the present net income from canal tolls, ample provision would be made to pay the interest of the debt promptly, and to extinguish the principal within the designated period, besides leaving a most abundant provision for working and repairing the canal, without resorting to taxation.

Mr. Hatch said that upon this plan the canal would, within two years, and at an expenditure of $3,000,000, be put in thoroughly good condition. This and the reduction of tolls would attract very large accessions of business, and enable the State of New-York to compete triumphantly with alien routes. They would effectually drain the commercial channels, through which trade is now increasingly diverted from us. Beyond this he looked forward to the time when the funded debt would be paid, and the State could reduce tolls to the minimum cost of working and repairing the canal; thus attaining the desirable ultimatum originally intended by its projectors—a free channel of trade, open to all comers, and reaching from the waters of the Ocean to those of the Great Lakes and the Mississippi.

He condemned the policy of procrastination and inaction as to the canals, comparing it to that of a landlord in good credit, but whose house is encumbered to a tithe of its value, who, when he might derive a good and increasing income, if he would make moderate repairs and changes, perversely refuses to take any warning from his declining revenue, while his property becomes more and more dilapidated, until the damages are irreparable, his income and his house are gone, but the mortgage and his personal responsibilities remain to be discharged.

He said it would be noticed, that although in the year recently closed, the movement of property from the West was unusually large, and exceeded that of any previous year, the income from tolls had decreased more than four hundred thousand dollars; and, if the returns of the last two calendar years were made the criterion, the actual decrease would be seen to be nearly seven hundred thousand dollars. He attributed this falling off to the unstatesmanlike views adopted in the administration of our canal affairs, and had no hesitation in saying that, if the present course were continued, the revenue would be reduced lower and lower, and the present debt, instead of being paid at the end of ten years, would never be extinguished without recourse to direct taxation of the people, who would also sustain a loss of over $20,000,000 invested in the canal traffic and in the means of transport.

If we are alive to our interests, and cheapen the cost of transportation, as far as we are able, we shall find that our share of the grain exporting trade of the United States is yet in its infancy. The Chicago merchants, eager to push their business, have, he was informed, already carried out their intention of placing samples of their various grades of flour in the rooms of the Corn Exchanges of several of the chief cities of Great Britain and Ireland, with the expectation that sales may be promoted to the mutual benefit of themselves and their customers.

The exportation of wheat and flour depends to a considerable extent on our making the greatest possible reduction in tolls. The Chicago Board of Trade in its latest report, demonstrates that until some relief is afforded eastward from Buffalo, there is little hope for any abatement in charges from Chicago to the Atlantic. The members of that Board who have made this subject the study of their lives, and are vitally interested in it, formally and officially warn us that "it is a proposition plain to any one who will examine the subject, that unless the State of New-York reduces the tolls on Western produce to a point that will merely pay the cost of repairs and expenses, her canals must ere many years, cease to be the great highway to market for those products." Basing their operations on sound statistical data, they point out that "it does not follow that when her business is diverted from her canals, it will be necessarily transferred to *her* railroads;" and emphatically warn us that other cities are actively competing for the business by rail—that even our water route has formidable competition.

He went on to say that the question of transportation was now attracting general attention. It should not be forgotten who pay its cost. It is not those who ride through the country in royal or imperial cars encompassed with a luxury that Queen Victoria or Louis Napoleon might envy, but the poor people, the consumers, the laboring millions. It is the freight traffic, not the passenger traffic, which pays the immense incomes to our railway corporations. This subject should be reflected upon before the canals are permitted to go into the hands of corporations. The railways have their proper freights, and let them carry them. The canals have their proper freights, and the railroads should keep their hands off from them. Still he made no war on railways. He believed in both. Cheap transit of property, with free competition over our canals, is one of the inalienable rights of the people, and the friends of the canal should insist upon retaining it for the public benefit, whatever may be the efforts of railway or other monopolists. By the low cost of freight on the various necessaries of life brought by way of the canal, many millions are annually saved to the masses of the people, and pauperism and taxation are incalculably diminished.

The value of modern means of co.nn unication is demonstrated by the rapidity of their growth. The first canal made in England does not date further back than 1755, and was only eleven miles in length.

In 1830 there were only twenty-three miles of railroad in the United States. By the end of the present year there will be in operation 50,000 miles of railroad, representing a capital of $2,200,000,000.

Mr. Hatch forcibly illustrated this part of his subject by instancing the New-York Central, which, only seventeen years ago, consisted of no less than ten independent links, connecting the Hudson with the Lakes. This combination now controls within the State of New-York, and under the direction of one man, 974 miles of track, represented by about $125,000,000 of paper securities, although the "private capital actually expended" was not more than $40,000,000. Practically, including other States, this combination represents nearly 5,000 miles of track and more than $300,000,000 of capital, according to the statement of Charles F. Adams, Sen., in a recent number of the *North American Review*. Mere figures could not represent the millions of property which the central directory of railway power controls. Colonel Benton, in a debate upon the moneyed power and acquisition of property by U. S. banks, said that when the French army marched upon Cairo, the officers asked the Egyptians, Who owns this palace? The reply was, The Mameluke. Who owns that large estate? The Mameluke. Mr. H. left to his hearers the application of this historical allusion. The capital of the United States banks to which Mr. Benton alluded was only $35,000,000, whereas that of the railroad power is at present $2,000,000,000.

He said the intention of our legislators was, that the smallest tax consistent with adequate remuneration to the owners of railroads should be charged for carrying freight. Thus, under the existing laws of the State, the managers of these incorporations could not, to use the words of Mr. Adams, divide more than ten per cent. on the hundred dollars they had paid in; but they could call that hundred dollars four hundred, and levy and divide ten per cent. on the whole amount. This was the object sought by watering the stock of the Central Railroad, and, with the same motive, that of the Erie was secretly increased, in the short period of twenty months, from $16,574,300 to $70,000,000—an addition of three hundred and twenty-two per cent. of mere "water." Similar transactions have taken place all over the country, until the railroads, as estimated by Mr. Adams, have 450,000 employés and an annual gross income of $100,000,000.

An incalculable loss is sustained by all the honest industries of the country through this vicious system, and the only direct check the people of New-York and the nation have upon further combinations and more extensive monopolies to raise the price of transportation, is the canal, which is open to all comers and under the control of the State, and regulates the cost of carriage throughout the East and West, and through the whole North, during the season of navigation.

Mr. Hatch stated that during the last summer he had a large foreign correspondence with our Ministers in France, Holland, Belgium, Great Britain and Russia, as well as with gentlemen who are largely engaged in canal transportation in those countries, as to the condition of the canals in Europe, and the policy pursued in regard to them. He had found much to confirm his views as to the most expedient policy for the State to adopt. In Russia, applying the principle adopted in France under Louis XIV. as to the canal of Languedoc, the toll laid upon vessels and their cargoes in passing through the canals, for thousands of miles, and over their thousands of miles of canals, is so light that the revenue thus derived is not sufficient to repair them, and the deficiency is made up from the public treasury.

So important did the statesmen of Belgium deem the canals

and water-courses which constitute the internal navigation of their country, that within the last forty years the Government has progressively concentrated them in its own hands, and special appropriations are annually made for the amelioration of the existing works, and even for the development of new channels of communication, as is fully shown by the official "Rapport décennal sur la situation administrative de la Belgique."

In England the canals are numerous, but short, as well as narrow and shallow. No tax is levied on them, except a light assessment called the land-tax, for the national government, and the same local taxes as on other property. Their system is essentially different from that of our own canals, as they belong to private companies. The lesson to be derived from their recent history is instructive. Their condition was of so much importance that a Royal commission was issued to inquire into it, and made an elaborate report in 1867. Mr. Hatch had learned from it that out of the 3,890 miles of inland navigation in England and Scotland, the ownership of nearly one-third had then already been amalgamated with that of railways. Previous to 1865, no less than 37 canals had been bought up and incorporated with railways, in the same way as the State canals of Pennsylvania had been bought by the Pennsylvania Central Railway. The people of Pennsylvania now have to pay every year, in the increased cost of the fuel they use, more than the whole sum paid to their State for its canals. The object of the English Railway Companies in thus purchasing the canals was to prevent competition and secure a monopoly in freight.

Authentic statements were made before the Commissioners, showing the heavy profits such companies made, after going to the enormous expense of buying up large sections of canals. Being thus enabled to monopolize the traffic, the companies skilfully raised the tolls, not in such an unnecessarily exorbitant degree as to bring their affairs into prominent notice, cover them with public odium, and draw upon them the interference of Parliament, but to a rate sufficiently high to exclude the competition of other forwarders or carriers upon them. It was found that such combinations never give to the community at large as good facilities as would be enjoyed if the canals were independent.

To so serious an extent were these amalgamations and monopolies carried, that laws were passed prohibiting them; except when sanctioned by a special Act of Parliament. Experience demónstrated that the public interests suffer whenever such acts are passed; and it was proved by ample testimony that a sound policy demanded that the canals should be kept open as highways to any one who chooses to carry on them, as they were in Great Britain until 1847 or 1848, and as they yet, thank God, are in this State. The fact was fully established that there is no permanent competition between railroads, or wherever they obtain power. In all such operations the public loses a salutary check upon exorbitant charges. Monopoly does not arise on the canals. They have this distinctive speciality, that their owners are not, as those of railways are, themselves carriers of the greater part of their traffic, but "are open, upon payment of toll, to the public, and not only to large carriers; any man who has capital enough to buy a boat and to pay the toll, which is a very small fraction of the total cost of conveyance, can carry upon the canal."

From whatever source Mr. H. had obtained information, the testimony left no doubt that wherever railroads and canals run between the same points and there is no amalgamation, the canals can compete favorably with the railways in the carriage of such articles as metals and minerals, generally, grain, flour and lumber, are heavy and bulky in proportion to their value, the effect which of speed being often of less consequence than the increase of cost in carriage by rail. So far are canals from being superseded by railroads, as was at one time supposed would be the case, that about 320 miles of canals are now projected to connect Berlin with Dresden and Frankfort.

In Holland steam is extensively used to propel boats on the canals. The engineer of the Belgian Towing Company writes, that by the use of steam on a canal of adequate dimensions, a reduction of 66 per cent. has been made in the charges for freight on a railway parallel to the canal.

One of the most extensive coal miners in England, who is practically well acquainted with the canals of his country, in a recent letter to Mr. Hatch, says: "On some canals they are using screw boats successfully, at a speed of about 4 to $4\frac{1}{2}$ miles an hour, and they do not at that rate injure the banks. Where railways have the control of a canal they do not encourage the use of steam on it; but in a level country, *where a canal has a fair depth of water, say six feet six inches to seven feet, with a sufficient width for vessels carrying* 150 *tons, they would successfully compete with railways except as regards light goods and passengers.* The use of the larger vessels greatly reduces the cost of transit. A small engine of 12 to 15 horse power will propel a barge carrying 120 tons of coal. Two men and a boy can navigate such a vessel."

The dimensions thus described indicate that steam may be profitably used on canals far smaller than the Erie would be with the contemplated improvements, and on boats much less than half the size it would admit. Other information shows that steam is most frequently used on such canals as are connected with rivers and estuaries corresponding to the Hudson River, the harbor of New-York and the terminus of the canal at Buffalo on the Lakes.

He said it is scarcely necessary to add, on this branch of the subject, that we are far behind the Europeans in improving our canals; and while they are extending their canal system, we are hesitating over the inauguration of a policy that would preserve those already constructed.

He said the policy of the friends of the canals is in the interest of the people, and to save them from taxation; and had no doubt that under a readjustment of the financial clause of the Constitution of 1846, and by the removal of the restrictions upon the power of the Canal Board to reduce tolls, in order to retain the trade of the canals, the public works can be improved and made free and self-sustaining, at no distant time, without any recourse to taxation. He was confident the funding policy is gaining ground, and had noticed lately that Peter B. Sweeney had been interviewed, by which is supposed to be meant turned inside out, and that he was found to be in favor of the improvement of the canals and low tolls; and many others might be mentioned.

He knew that William M. Tweed presented, last Winter, in the State Senate, resolutions in the interest of the canal improvements, and approved of them. Senator Murphy also presented resolutions from the New-York Produce Exchange, recommending an amendment to relieve the Canal Board from the unreasonable and obsolete restrictions of the Constitution of 1846, and vigorously advocated immediate action on them, remarking that there somewhere should be statesmanship enough in our administration to redeem our canals from the anomalous condition of having plenty of money, but being debarred from using it for necessary improvements, and the Canal Board from being restrained from reducing the tolls to meet the diversion of our trade.

Mr. Hitchman, the present Speaker in the Assembly, supported the same proposals, in one of the most brilliant and comprehensive speeches ever uttered in that House. These gentlemen belong to a live institution, called Tammany, and will never consent to be tied to a dead carcase, like the Constitution of 1846.

Governor Hoffman, who is a progressive man, has, in his Message, taken bold ground in favor of free commerce over our canals, and must be in favor of any measure that will improve and save them.

The Albany *Argus* had already expressed itself in favor of funding the canal debt, and many of the most able lawyers of the State had agreed with the plan. The *Argus* was very emphatic in defining its position, and said:

"*We see no way of a speedy reduction of tolls on the canals except by funding the present canal debt, giving it eighteen years to run. In that way the tolls might be reduced to a low figure. And if the revenues should be decreased, it would produce no immediate embarrassment, as the annual amount required to pay the debt would be lessened on account of the lengthening of the time of payment.*"

Even our mutual friend Greeley, whom Mr. Hatch had once heard in the Constitutional Convention make his proposal in favor of selling the canals, had been converted, and recently, in a lecture at Buffalo, had said that for every million the State of New-York had expended upon her canals, she had received one hundred millions back again in return. Although the conversion of Mr. Greeley to the support of this sound, economical doctrine was tardy, yet his accession should be hailed as that of a representative of a great party in our State and nation, and of a most valuable champion of the rights and welfare of the people. As a supporter of the canal, we should welcome him, if from no other reason, from a due consideration of that saving clause to which many of us must ultimately resort, to the effect, that although it is hard for old sinners to repent, it is never too late.

There is a labyrinth of constitutional and financial difficulties; but where there is a will there is a way, and a way should be and can be found out of this difficulty. The speaker said he would cordially support any plan by which the result he aimed at could be secured, and maintained that it is not enough for those who oppose any great measure of acknowledged public utility to raise cavils and objections to every policy that may be suggested to carry it out, unless they accompany their objections with proposals of better plans for the attainment of the results admitted to be desirable. He compared them to men who would pull down a house where it was needed, but could not build another in its place. It was essential to the character of a statesman that he should not only be able to destroy, but also to construct or build up. He said the remarks of those staunch and sagacious statesmen, Clinton and Morris, in reply to the opponents of the canal in their day, are as applicable now as they were then. Speaking of the opposition they encountered, they said:

"The Commissioners must, nevertheless, have the hardihood to brave the sneers and sarcasms of men who, with too much pride to study and too little intellect to think, undervalue what they do not understand, and condemn what they cannot comprehend. Wise legislators will examine and reason upon facts."

He expressed an undoubting conviction that by the adoption of the policy proposed, the former trade would be restored to the State and the nation. Our water highways are in a critical condition, and something must be done for their preservation. The diversion of trade had commenced, and would go on if no means were adopted to check it. It was like a *crevasse* in the banks of the Mississippi, and, if neglected, would widen and deepen till the whole carrying trade of the West would be carried away from us.

SPEECH OF E. E. DAVIS, Esq.

MR. PRESIDENT—This large assemblage of earnest business men of the State of New-York are here to-day to consult together in relation to the administration of the affairs of our canals. Our great system of internal improvements was projected and constructed to develop the resources of our State, and to promote and protect the industrial interests of all our citizens.

The hopes of the men who originated our system of internal improvements have been more than realized. The development of the resources of the Empire State, and the prosperity of our citizens, have been without a parallel. And now that other and competing channels for transportation have been opened up, it is of more importance than ever before that the canals of the State, which are the property of the people, should be put and kept in good navigable condition. The West demands cheap transportation for her products to market, and the people of the whole East are alike interested. They demand that the cost of what they eat and wear shall not be increased on account of the negligence and carelessness of canal officials, nor the corruption and rascality of contractors. We do not undertake to charge that all contractors are dishonest. Some there are who do their work well, and perform their contracts in good faith; but the general rule is the reverse.

Since 1854 the canals of the State have been repaired and improved under a system known as the "Repair Contract System." The business men here claim that the working of that system has failed to protect the interests of the people, has failed to keep the canals in navigable condition; and notwithstanding the large sums which have been drawn from the people by direct taxation to repair and improve, decay and ruin mark the whole line of the public works to-day.

You may compare the expenditures upon the canals for the last five years for ordinary repairs, extraordinary repair, improvement work, grants by the Legislature to contractors as extra compensation, and awards by the Canal Appraisers, in many instances for damages on account of the negligence of contractors, and you will find that the total expenditure for your canals will greatly exceed the expenditures of the same number of years under the old Superintendent system.

The Auditor, in his report, states the expenses of the canals for the past year to be $1,278,507.52. He does not give the amount paid for extraordinary repairs, improvements and extra compensation, by the Legislature, nor the awards by the Canal Appraisers. When all these amounts are paid, you will find the total expenses of your canals are nearly or quite two millions of dollars.

The State Engineer, in his report, says that the amount of work done under the supervision of the Engineer is $1,463,843.85. His statement shows $185,336.33 more work done than the Auditor has paid for, and he does not include the Legislative grants to contractors, nor the awards of the Appraisers for damages.

By an examination of the Canal Commissioners' reports you will find statements for ordinary, extraordinary and improvement work; also, the amounts awarded by the Canal Appraisers for damages, but appropriations made by the Legislature to contractors for extra services are not stated. For the year ending September 30, 1868, the whole expenses of the canals were $1,727,000; for 1867, September 30, $2,124,086.66; and for September 30, 1866, $1,733,000; and for September 30, 1865, $2,222,261.00; calling the past year's expenditure, as stated by the Engineer, $1,473,000, and we have the total cost for our canals for the last five years $9,279,347.61, saying nothing about what the Legislature has done for the poor contractors.

If you will examine the Commissioners' reports for 1850-51-52-53 and '54, the years when there was the most complaint with regard to the corruptions of the Superintendent system, you will find the total expenses for repairs to the canals for the five years to be $3,799,000.

It is said that for the last four years there has been a large amount of improvement work done. Let us examine this improvement matter. For the first ten years under the contract system the towing path was not graded and kept up, the docking rotted down and was not replaced, the slope walls were not repaired, and bridges and structures were in general dilapidation; appropriations were obtained for extraordinary and improvement work. The contracts were let to the same parties who had the repair contracts, and whenever the towing path has been repaired or graded the improvement fund has paid for the work. If walls are fallen in, a slight change by the Engineer in charge of the slope, width or foundation, and it becomes new work; and it now requires only to remove the abutment of a bridge from six to twelve inches, and the span is increased so much that the contractor is excused from repairing or building, and the improvement fund pays for work the contractor should perform.

Almost the entire repairs to the Champlain Canal have been done from the extraordinary repair, and improvement fund, for the last five years. Within that time there has been appropriated some $700,000 to improve this canal; and, exclusive of three or four locks which have been rebuilt, over one-half of the balance of the fund has been used to pay for work the contractor should have done in pursuance of his contract.

The Auditor, in his report, cites Section 1 of the Champlain Canal. He says that section had been let to a responsible party from March 1st, 1868, for four years and ten months, at an annual compensation of $29,400. That the Superintendent had been allowed to take possession of this section against the earnest protest of this much injured and responsible contractor, and in three and one-half months expended $53,743.30. Let us examine the facts in relation to this section, and see whether they sustain the position of the Auditor in favor of the contract system.

This same contractor had this section previous to 1868. The towing path of this section had been graded in 1867-8. New dock sticks had been placed upon the towing path bank, but all that was done was paid for from the improvement fund, and any work he could not get paid for out of that fund he did not do. The navigation of that section had been getting from bad to worse during the whole time this contractor had been upon it. His attention was called in the fall of 1868 to the condition of the Fort Miller dam across the North River; unless it was repaired a portion of it would go out. He paid no attention to the warning. His attention was again called in the spring to this dam and to the general condition of the section. A portion of the improvement work of the year before had fallen into the canal; numerous sand bars from small streams had been formed, and the condition of the section was generally dilapidated. A committee of business men went over the section and reported its condition to the Commissioner, the late Oliver Bascom. He immediately directed his Superintendent to go over the section and make an estimate of the cost of the repairs necessary to secure navigation. The estimates were made and signed by the Commissioner, and duly presented to the Auditor. The contractor was notified to commence the work. He refused, and the Superintendent took charge of the section and did the work under the direction of the Commissioner, and that section of the canal was put in condition for once, and the first time in five years; and some twenty thousand dollars or more of this contractor's money was expended upon this section. In the meantime, and about the opening of the canal, the freshet had taken away about 80 to 100 feet of the dam across the North River, which feeds the sixteen mile level. If the Commissioner had waited for the water to run down before he repaired the break, he could do the work cheaper, but navigation would have to be suspended, and the whole business interests would have sustained almost an irreparable loss. He directed cribs to be sunk and the repairs to be made before the water run down. Some fifteen thousand dollars were expended in repairing a break in the dam which never would have occurred if this contractor had done his duty in the early spring or fall before; but navigation was secured for the whole time by the prompt action of the Commissioner. Other damages were done by the same freshet on this section which were promptly repaired, and helped to make up the amount of $53,000. This contractor finding the Commissioner was determined to make him perform his work according to contract abandoned the section. This same man boasts that he runs the Democratic party, and owns the Legislature; that he could get appropriations as fast as Bascom could spend them, and while his section was being put in repair, he was in Albany before the Legislature, and did get an appropriation for work which he never performed, about equal to what it had cost to put the section in repair by the Superintendent, and at the same time, and in the same bill, had the North River dam and the Mohawk dam cut off from his repair section. All the money expended on that section on account of the freshet could have been prevented if this contractor had done his duty. Necessary repair in the spring would have prevented the disaster, and any disposition shown on his part to put his section in repair, and perform his contract in good faith, and the Commissioner would never have put the Superintendent in charge. This section was managed by the Superintendent until about September 1st, and navigation was kept up better than it had ever been before.

It was re-let about September 1st for some $19,000. It was then in good repair. This new contractor undertook to run the section without help, without watchmen, and without any police regulation to look after the interests of the people. The result was the severe rains filled the levels to overflowing and the banks were washed away, and navigation was suspended on this canal for twenty-eight days in the month of October, on account of this break and one that occurred on Section 3, between Fort Ann and Fort Edward. This section was in charge of the Auditor's responsible contractor. There was no freshet at the time the break occurred at Fort Ann. The repairs on Section 1 were finished, and the water was let into the whole line. The Twelve Mile Level at Fort Ann filled to overflowing; even the lock gates at Fort Ann would have drawn off the surplus water. They were not opened, not a waste weir was turned. The water commenced coming in at six o'clock at night, and by six o'clock in the morning it was running over the bank, and a break occurred that delayed navigation eight to ten days; making a loss to navigation of almost the entire month of October, and the whole people suffered a loss which can hardly be estimated.

A majority of the breaks and delays that have occurred upon the canals of the State for the past five years, can be charged directly to the contract system. Contractors do not put men on to watch the levels and keep the water in control; and if the Commissioner puts on a Superintendent or an Engineer who is desirous of doing his duty, and protecting the interests of the people, the contractors will either corrupt him, or villify and defame him until they drive him off the work. They must get rid of him or control him. Contractors say whether work shall be done under their contracts, or whether it is extraordinary or improvement work. They lay out the work and make the estimates, and after the work is done in the most temporary manner, they make out the estimates, and their "tools" sign their names and the money is drawn from the Auditor. If there is any danger of competition they will take the contract at a lower figure than any honest man can do the work, relying upon the "tools" to lay out and measure the work as they direct, or their ability to go to the Legislature and obtain a grant for extra compensation.

Gentlemen, the contract system is a failure, except to enrich the contractor. Every business interest of the people, dependent upon canal navigation, is depressed. Capital invested in products, grain, iron ore and lumber does not pay on account of the vexatious delay and increased cost of transportation. Put the canals in good navigable condition the size they now are, and you will decrease the cost of transportation 33 per cent., and increase the business of the canals more than an equal amount; and then a reduction of tolls of 25 per cent. will produce more revenue than the canals now pay; but we do not want revenue except to keep the canals in repair. The benefit to individuals from cheap and quick transit of property is all the revenue we ask. The canals are for the people and not the State.

If business men are united the remedy is in their hands. The Democratic party is pledged to repeal the repair contract system, and all the contracts now held under it. The men who organized and perfected this scheme of plunder, and who have controlled the Canal Board and Legislature for the last ten years, and ruined the Republican party, are now making an effort to control the Legislature and to retain this system which has robbed the people of millions of money.

United effort and prompt action on the part of business men, before the Legislature, and we can secure a plan or policy of canal management which will protect the interests of the whole people.

SPEECH OF Hon. HENRY L. FISH.

Mr. President and Gentlemen of the Convention of The Commercial Union of the State of New-York:

Although it is getting late, and the grounds of our grievances and complaints against the past and present canal management, and the remedies for them at this most critical time of our canals, have been pretty well covered and argued by the able gentlemen who have preceded me, yet I desire to say something with reference to canal management.

I shall endeavor to be brief, and detain you but a short time.

The main, and I may say the sole, object of The Commercial Union, was and is the maintainance and protection of our canals and the canal system, and to prevent the inroads upon the good navigation of our canals. This Union is *non partisan;* it is composed of public spirited, determined men of and from all parties, who have large and comprehensive views; men who *cannot* be bought or sold like cattle in the market; men who have banded and are banding themselves together with firm and solemn resolve to rescue our canals from the hands of supine officers and from corrupt and unscrupulous contractors—officers and contractors who have shown by their past acts and the present alarming condition of the canals an unfitness to be longer trusted or tolerated. They have brought the canals into disrepute; they have lessened to an alarming degree the receipts into the treasury, as they are increasing their drafts upon said treasury without returning an equivalent. They are destroying and driving the carrying trade from our State and to competing railroad lines. They are ruining the commercial men who are engaged in the carrying trade, and the commerce of the canals. They have destroyed the confidence of the great and boundless West in our canals, whose people are seeking other safer and more reliable routes of transit. They are, as before said, driving away the commerce of the canals, and have nearly destroyed our proud commercial supremacy. Give any man or the public an exposition of the condition the canals are now in, and none but men who navigate them and know from actual experience will believe you, it is so incredible. No one knows but those who are engaged in the carrying trade, how much forwarders and boatmen suffer, and how much the State is the loser, by reason of this disgraceful and corrupt contract system and the want of navigation.

One of the sources of great delays and loss to boatmen and the State is the sale by contractors, and in some instances by the officers themselves, of water for milling and manufacturing purposes, between Buffalo and Troy. I can furnish positive and irrefragable evidence of water being sold and drawn from the canal in open daylight, while boats were laying on the ground for hours and even days anchored in the mud, and hundreds of thousands of dollars have been lost by those navigating the canals by this system of corruption and the theft of the State waters. Is there no remedy?

At Syracuse, the Salt Works and the millers use the water from the canal, every drop of which is needed to keep up good navigation. Locktenders each side of said city sell the water to the millers, and receive flour by the barrel from time to time for drawing the water into pit levels for their use. This is well known, and the fact admitted by contractors, and even by the Auditor—while boats lay aground each side of the city, where the canal has not been bottomed out to any extent for years. Again, we ask, is there no remedy, no relief from these outrages?

Our boats are left to drag their slow lengths along over sand bars and in shallow water, and are consequently detained, and occupy the time, and are at the expense of two trips to get the proceeds of one, and, in some instances, at the time and expense of three trips for the avails of one.

Oh! what a state of things to be tolerated by the intelligent people of our noble State!

Why, Mr. President, the losses by this system of management to individual men and the State are really appalling. It is worse than the deadly upas: it is withering and drying up the sources of our wealth and pride. Look, sir, at the condition of the main trunk—the bottom filled up in innumerable places with mud. Look at the old-fashioned and rickety lock-gates, through which immense quantities of water are rushing at the rate of three miles an hour. A change must be made. The losses by the State, forwarders and boatmen are counted by the million each succeeding year. And that is not the worst—our State is losing the carrying trade, which is its life's blood. This management and delays have driven millions worth of property through channels outside of the State, and to competing railroad lines that contribute no tolls to the State.

This is a progressive age. Our State is far behind the times; she has been retrograding. Our canals are not as serviceable now, nor have they the capacity they had ten years ago. I know it by experience, and so says State Engineer Richmond, who is the best of authority. Contractors are careless and indifferent, and do not watch their sections; and when a breach takes place they manage to let it enlarge, so that the cost of repairs exceeds their contract, and enables them to get a good large slice from the public crib for extra work.

Again, Mr. President, I ask, when will the people apply the proper remedy and save to themselves the thousand miles of canals which has been the source of so much pride and advantage to the States? This infernal system, so degrading, so expensive, so disastrous, so destructive, must be "wiped out" and extinguished forever.

As a sample, look at the Pool Brook break which was leaking eight or ten days prior to giving out. Word was sent to the contractor, by various persons, but not the least attention was paid to it. Four feet of the outside of the towpath, for two rods long, had settled to the water's edge, and the water was oozing up through the towpath from the canal and running into the field below, and finally gave way and caused eight day's detention, a dead stop, and after being repaired, ten days more to clean away the crowd of boats. No men there, or near; his boat was loaned out and on the Black River Canal, and this break alone cost the Companies to which I belong ten thousand dollars.

Again, I ask, is there no remedy for these awful calamities to boatmen, and *tremendous* and *double* loss to the People of the State? Does and must corruption rule the hour? There was a series of breaks that followed in quick succession after the Pool Brook, viz: A Culvert two miles below Coxes, Fort Plain Aqueduct, Canajoharie Aqueduct, Spraker's Aqueduct, Yankee Hill Lock Culvert, Seven Mile Level; Seven Mile Level Culvert, and Hoffman's Ferry Aqueduct. What terrible and telling disasters these were; some of which, it is fair to presume, could not have been avoided; but it is known that others might, if attention had been given to the structures in time. It is also fair to say that some of the contractors worked well and hurried up the repairs, but some did not, and everybody said, the Auditor included, great delays were experienced consequent upon bad and willful management of others. That the public were outraged by it, and by one *Donaldson* in particular, whose actions and management was, to say the least, most reprehensible. These breaks were appalling and wonderfully disastrous to boatmen and the people. It brought to a dead stand, each side of these breaks, nearly all the boats navigating the Erie and lateral Canals. It congregated at least five thousand horses, and cost the Companies alone, with whom I am interested, thirty thousand dollars.

Again, I ask, is there no relief? This contract system is antagonistic to the interest of the people and the State. There has such an antagonism grown up, by reason of this outrageous management, between the managers and the men that navigate the canals that this alone is sufficient cause to abolish the odious system. I know it will be hard work to do it. But, Mr. President, it must be done, and we are bound to do it. We must have good and responsible officers. Put the responsibility upon them, and have them put the canals in order; bottom them out seven feet; make canals, as intended, broad and deep; modernize and improve the lock gates so that they will hold water and can be opened *easily* and *quickly*. It now takes one and two men, and sometimes a horse, to open the gates, they are so old and rickety, and the water running through the upper ones at the rate of three miles an hour, creates a pressure against the lower gates, which not only lengthens the time to lock boats, but wastes the water that is so much needed to keep up navigation; but, worst of all, it creates far greater detention to loaded boats that tow into them against a three mile current which, together with the current made by the displacement of the water as the boat enters the lock, creates a great resistance as she enters the lock; lengthens the time it takes to lock boats; besides, it drags and strains teams to an alarming extent.

Again, Mr. President and Gentlemen, I ask, is there no remedy? Must the canals be lost? Must the men who have spent their lifetime in the trade of the canals be ruined, and the earnings of forty years lost and frittered away for the sake of enriching a smaller number of men who return no equivalent?

Mr. President, I ask is it the policy of our State to allow their public works to be used in the building up and enriching one or two hundred officials and contractors at the expense and downfall of fifty thousand commercial men and boatmen, and the total destruction of the grandest of all public works, which has built up the State of New-York; which has built up and carried the great City of New-York, which is the just pride of the State, to her proud position as the great commercial emporium of the world, and which has built up the great and growing West, that still clings to us and has a feeling and interest with, and allied to us by commercial ties and a feeling of reciprocity, and which is daily crying unto the people of this State to rescue and save our canals, and reciprocate and fraternize with them for the mutual benefit and aggrandizement of the State of New-York and all the West?

I call upon all within the sound of my voice to unite with us to rescue, retain and maintain our common inheritance, and the proud commercial supremacy of the State. I call upon the Legislature to act; to abolish the odious system; to place the responsibility of repairs and the maintainance of the canals in competent and safe hands, and have the canals put in order, to make the channels wide and deep. We demand the protection and perpetuity and efficiency of our canals, for present use and for all future generations. The men who come here are public spirited men. They come here on a labor of love. They come at their own expense, for the public good. There is enough in that to give us great hope and courage. I want every Democrat and every Republican to think of this subject, and come to the rescue. I have always been taught that it was a good thing to have the Lord on our side; and when Mr. Lord was nominated for State Senator from our district, well knowing that he had been identified with this contract system, I propounded to him some questions, and will now read them and his reply to you, to show you where he stands:

MR. FISH TO MR. LORD.

ROCHESTER, *Oct.* 30, 1869.

"*Hon Jarvis Lord, Rochester:*

DEAR SIR—The Democratic party have put you in nomination for the high and most important office of State Senator. Well knowing that you have been heretofore engaged as a canal contractor on our canals under a system which as carried on, seems to be most disastrous and deleterious to the people of our State, and the abolition of which, in the sound judgment of very many of the best men in the State, is imperatively demanded; and it being patent to every observer that the canals under the present policy are badly managed, by reason of which the commercial supremacy of the State is being frittered away, and that the present is a most critical period, requiring prompt and effective action to secure the reform demanded,—it is desirable for us to know what course you will pursue should you be elected; therefore we ask :

1st, Will you go for the abolition of the contract system?
2d, Will you favor and do what you can to put and keep the canals in good and complete navigable order?
3d, Will you do all you can to foster and encourage the trade and commerce of the canals?
4th, Will you do all you can legitimately to protect and retain the carrying trade, and the commercial supremacy of our State, against the unscrupulous monopolies who are seeking by all kinds of appliances to divert trade from the State?

Truly yours,
HENRY L. FISH."

Mr. LORD'S REPLY.

ROCHESTER, *Oct.* 30, 1869.
"*Hon. Henry L. Fish:*

DEAR SIR—Your note of this date making inquiry as to the course I shall pursue if elected to represent this district in the State Senate, has just been received I reply in the affirmative to your several questions. The Democratic party, of which you and I are members, holds a clearly defined position in harmony with the objects you have in view. As a member of the last Democratic Assembly I voted for the bill to abolish the contract system which passed that body, and if now elected to the Senate I shall feel bound to support and vote for any kindred measure that may be deemed advisable, and that may be approved by my party associates. I shall esteem it a duty to heartily co-operate with my Democratic colleagues upon any and all propositions looking to the successful management and navigation of our canals, to the welfare of all interested in their commerce, and to the maintenance of the proud supremacy of New-York in the carrying trade.

I remain, very respectfully, yours, etc.,
JARVIS LORD."

Mr. President, by this you will see that we have "the Lord on our side," and are bound to succeed. Our Union is in earnest. Already our members are numbered by the thousand, and radiate all over the State, and we "mean business." We are bound to redeem and save our canals. The Union has started for the rescue, and will fight to the bitter end. "We will not give up the ship," but will fight to the last; and if we fail, we will die as did the glorious Union boys on the sinking Cumberland, fighting up through the water to the last.

I had a conference with the Auditor a few days since. He complained of the boatmen, and said they were troublesome. Who can blame men for feeling as the boatmen do, who are kept weeks, and I may say months, on the passage from Buffalo to Troy for want of a canal? Why, Mr. President, I have started young men, in the prime of their lives, with boats and cargoes for New York, and when they returned they had grown as gray as myself, and had raised large families of children.

The Auditor complained that boats were too long in transit between Buffalo and Troy, just as though that was a fault of ours. He said we should go through in seven days. That is just what we want to do, and will do if you will give us a canal. But at present, if we go from Buffalo to Troy, as the canal now is, in even in double that time, we must take the overland route.

Why, Mr. President, we were detained above Lockport by the freshet, caused by high water in Tonawanda Creek, in September, for eight days, simply because the contractor had allowed the guard gates to become so rotten that he dare not shut them, for fear they would not stand the pressure. The water which flowed through them, and inundated Lockport Locks, and caused a dead stoppage eight days of three or four hundred boats, was a most severe loss. Still, we have *no relief, no remedy.*

Again, on the 1st of December there was another freshet, which stopped boats for 36 hours, just as the ice was forming, which again cost the boatmen caught there between three and four thousand dollars.

The Commercial Union was formed for, and is determined to, cause an immediate reform. " We have many outriders." " Coming events cast their shadows before them." We are on the war path, and ere long the fur will fly, and the contractors too.

In conclusion, we appeal to the whole people to come forward and join us in this great work. We ask them to join us in this crusade against corruption, against robbery, against fraud, against the destruction of our canals; against each and every man or officer who is devoid of integrity, who is incompetent, who is not equal to the obligation and duties that devolve upon him, against repair contractors, against every man whose long and slimy fingers are reaching for the public crib, and who for the money he receives returns no equivalent.

We call earnestly upon all those who are for maintaining with honest fidelity the dignity of the State, and the protection of the State Canals, and who are willing to work with assiduity and indomitable tenacity and perseverance to bring them back to their former usefulness, retaining and maintaining their prestige, and the proud commercial supremacy of the carrying trade.

Gentlemen, I thank you for the interest with which you have listened to me in these hasty remarks, upon these most interesting and important subjects, with which the whole people are so intimately connected and allied.

SPEECH OF Hon. CHARLES STANFORD.

Mr. President, and Gentlemen of the Convention:

It was not my purpose to say anything, and I am now before you through the President, who introduced me against my earnest desire.

But as I am to speak, I will do so boldly. I shall not, like the Honorable gentleman who addressed you this morning, refrain from saying anything against persons or party, but shall state facts, let them hit where they may. As I have been somewhat identified in the work of showing up some of the frauds connected with the management of the canals, it may not be out of place for me to speak of a case that came under my observation, and which I think will give you some light as to the manner in which things are done.

In the course of my legislative duties I learned that a prolific cause of plunder existed; and that great frauds were perpetrated about the canals, under the head of new work, or a change of plan. The repair contractor agrees, and is bound by contract to keep not only in good repair his section, but to rebuild and restore all structures that wear out or decay. Hence it becomes necessary to rebuild walls, bridges, &c., whenever their condition shall require it. This is the proper work for the contractor. It is in fact almost all he has to do, and yet he does not do it. From some cause or other a bill is introduced in the Legislature authorizing the Canal Commissioners to build certain iron bridges to take the places where the old wooden structures are worn out; also to construct vertical, where slope walls must be repaired; and to do something of a different character where a repair is necessary that will change the plan of the work, and come in under the head of extraordinary repairs, for which an *extraordinary price* is to be paid; relieving the repair contractor from doing the work contemplated by the terms of his contract. But this is not all. The Board of Canal Commissioners kindly construe this operation and agree with the repair contractor of the section upon which the work is to be done, as to the price, and award him the work without competition.

Now it was to stop this mode of plunder, that I engrafted into a bill of appropriations this section, which, if the Convention please, I will read.

SEC. 3. "No part or portion of the moneys herein appropriated for new work shall be expended or paid, nor shall any contract involving such expenditure and payment be made on behalf of the State, until the maps, plans and estimates for such new work shall have been submitted to and approved by the Canal Board, and the work shall be advertised and let to the lowest bidder."

I supposed as did others, that this section would be effective. Let us see. I read from the record, and they cannot therefore deny it.

At a meeting of the Board of Canal Commissioners, held at their office, in the City of Albany, on Thursday, September 3, 1868. Present, S. T. Hayt and John D. Fay.

The following named proposals which were received at the Canal Commissioner's office in Schenectady, on the 1st instant, were opened and canvassed:

Iron Bridge at Washington and George Street, Rome.

Alexander J. Brown	$6,604 00
E. B. Van Dusen	5,535 70
J. A. Nichols	6,550 00
M. H. Mills	8,051 40
C. J. DeGraw	8,951 00
R. Conners	8,602 00

Iron Bridge at Port Jackson.

Alexander J. Brown	$2,589 62
E. B. Van Dusen	2,580 75
M. H. Mills	3,896 00
Munsell & Neff	2,993 75
C. J. DeGraw	6,497 00
R. Conners	2,625 75

Iron Bridge at Schuylerville.

Alexander J. Brown	$2,949 62
Willard Johnson	3,710 75
E. B. Van Dusen	2,668 37
M. H. Mills	3,365 25
Munsell & Neff	3,655 00
R. Conners	3,234 12

Iron Bridge at East Street, Fort Edward.

Alexander J. Brown	$2,078 87
Willard Johnson	2,976 75
E. B. Van Dusen	1,940 75
M. H. Mills	4,315 00
Munsell & Neff	2,533 75
C. J. DeGraw	5,185 00
R. Conners	2,238 37

At a meeting of the Board of Canal Commissioners, held at their office, in the City of Albany, on Friday, September 4, 1868. Present, R. C. Dorn and John D. Fay.

The following preamble and resolution was adopted:

By Mr. Fay,

Whereas, The Canal Board has informally advised the Canal Commissioners, not to let by contract, the rebuilding of Bridges under change of plan authorized by the Legislature by special Acts, but require the Repair Contractors to do the same under their several Repair Contracts, and allow them therefor the extra cost of the same, over and above the cost of rebuilding them on the original plan, therefore

Resolved, That no awarding of the work for constructing bridges at Rome, Port Jackson, Schuylerville and Fort Edward, for which proposals were received at Schenectady, on the 1st day of September, 1868, is deemed necessary. Adopted.

It will be seen, on examination, that the Board of Canal Commissioners did take the same view of this section that the Legislature did, and proceeded to advertise on plans, specifications, &c., and did receive proposals, and adjourn over, taking breath for renewed action. Subsequently they met, and the whereas comes in, setting forth the informal opinion of the Canal Board. And why did this Board give this informal opinion? What was it for? What end did they seek to accomplish? Surely they could not have been in collusion with the contractors. Gentlemen of the Convention, I prefer to throw around them the mantle of charity, and to believe that they gave this informal opinion unwittingly. The Canal Commissioners being thus fortified, the Board went to work in earnest. The result we have—twelve thousand dollars, the full amount of the appropriation, being given to Mr. Nichols for work at Rome, while the lowest bid was five thousand five hundred and thirty-five dollars and seventy cents, and that of Nichols himself, the Repair Contractor, but six thousand five hundred and fifty dollars; and yet this Board gave to Mr. Nichols twelve thousand dollars, the full amount of the appropriation. Luckily there was a limit.

At Port Jackson the lowest bid was two thousand five hundred and eighty dollars and seventy-five cents. Munsell & Neff, the repair contractors, bid two thousand nine hundred and ninety-three dollars and seventy-five cents, and they were given this bridge at six thousand dollars, the full amount appropriated—six thousand dollars, when the parties themselves only asked two thousand nine hundred and ninety-three dollars and seventy-five cents!

At Schuylerville the lowest bid was two thousand six hundred and sixty-eight dollars and thirty-seven cents. The bid of Willard Johnson, the repair contractor, was three thousand seven hundred and ten dollars and seventy-five cents, and yet, strange as it may appear, the work was awarded to Willard Johnson, at the enormous sum of seven thousand dollars, the full amount of the appropriation!

This is not all; but enough.

What shall we say of it? Do you understand it? Do you see it as it is? Is it not robbery, bold, bare-faced robbery, to give these men twice as much as they themselves asked? saying nothing about the lower bids for the same work by other parties? It would be robbery in an agent of mine, and I would treat him accordingly, and so would you.

This is but a sample of what is going on from day to day under this inefficient, profligate and plundering system of keeping the canals in repair by contract. There is comparatively nothing done except under this head of repairs extraordinary, paid out of a fund raised by direct tax yearly to the amount of about one million five hundred thousand dollars, and how this sum is expended, in part, and which is a fair sample, I have just told you.

The Auditor says in his report, that the contracting system for repairs is cheaper than the Superintendent system. It is not true, and he knows it, for he does not tell you of the large amount of money expended under the head of extraordinary repairs, but which money goes virtually for ordinary repairs. I may say something about the Auditor, as I helped to make him, and feel that I ought to tell why. We were much in want of an Auditor, and could not get the one we desired, and proposed to do the best we could. Mr. Bell's name was mentioned *as the coming man.*

I instituted some inquiries among those who knew him at home, and knowing that when in the Constitutional Convention as a member of the Sub-Committee of the Canal Committee, he reported an article favoring a Superintendent system, I deemed it best, as did those who acted with me, that his nomination should be confirmed. But we were sold. The first opportunity that offered, he came forward and appeared in Legislative caucus, where the subject under consideration was the repeal of the contracting system, when but one vote out of sixteen Republicans was required to accomplish it. I have no hesitation in saying that I believe that but for him that vote would have been had, yes, more than one, and the odious system forever disposed of.

But, gentlemen, he did not stop here. Last winter he got up a counter bill to continue the system, only making it more obnoxious still, and had the audacity to come and ask me to take it—present it as my own—saying at the same time that I had accomplished my purpose, and that it would be a good thing for me.

I ask, gentlemen, what sort of a man must he be, and what caused his sudden conversion from a friend of the superintendent system to a champion of the contract system? I leave you to answer, for it is hardly prudent in me.

Well, this bill of his, having been tendered to several, was finally brought up by being introduced in the Assembly through the then Chairman of the Canal Committee, reported, and permitted to sleep the remainder of the session. They dare not move it lest it should be amended so as to make it conform to the Senate bill. All this time the Auditor was not idle. Member after member was seen by him, frequently being sent for until the advanced day in the session rendered it impossible to accomplish anything.

I tell you, gentlemen, you have much to do, a hard work to perform, for these men of the ring are rich, and they boast that they make legislators; and whether they do or not, I know that the Canal Committee of the House could not have been *more* had they made every member of it. Why, Mr. President and gentlemen of the Convention, this committee locked up the Senate bill so closely that it could not be found for months after the Legislature had adjourned, and that, too, when it was their duty to return it, that it might go to the House where it originated. Hence I say it will be a difficult job to get rid of the system and the existing contracts, and unless you get rid of existing contracts you do not get rid of the system.

As to the future of our canals, I believe we should first get rid of the system of repairs by contract; second, finish them in accordance with the enlarged plan, which will cost between two and three millions of dollars. These two things being done, they will be kept in repair for about one-half of the present cost. You will then have twice the capacity that you now have, through the efficiency of management and enlargement, thereby making the canals afford a much larger revenue—consequently popular with the people, and virtually bringing you reduced tolls and all else that may be really desirable.

SPEECH OF DAVID J. MITCHELL, OF SYRACUSE.

I did not intend to offer any remarks to the Convention, for which I am not well prepared, and I will not delay the proceedings by speaking at length upon a subject which has brought such a numerous and respectable assemblage together in council. My sentiments and plans are chiefly embodied in the resolutions I have had the honor of reporting; no man can be more profoundly impressed with a sense of the vices and faults of our canal system, than I am myself. I have been employed in a service, where its iniquities have been exposed to my gaze and abhorrence, and where a moral conviction of other and still greater enormities, not known to, or suspected by the people, has been irresistibly forced upon my cognizance. The administration of the public works had become rotten and corrupt to the last degree, and exerted a most pernicious influence upon the officials connected with them, and upon political issues that have agitated and swayed our citizens. The corruptions that grow out of our canal management, have culminated, under the Contract Repair System, and if we would redeem the canals from inevitable ruin, purify again the halls of legislation, and expel the pestilential atmosphere in which the people are compelled to draw their breath, we must go right down into the depths of this sink of abominations, and exterminate the blood-suckers, to which it has given birth, and who now rule the State and enrich themselves by the plunder of its treasury.

We, who are here in attendance to-day, have not come here as partizans—as politicians seeking a new issue upon which to climb into power. We are Republicans and Democrats, to be sure; we could scarce be anything else. But I believe every gentleman present is actuated by a sincere and patriotic desire to make one effort for rescuing the canals from the grasp of the spoilers. On this question we can strike hands together, and make a common cause; we can unite and act in harmony.

I have listened with great pleasure to the address of Gov. Seymour, as I have no doubt my own friends and the friends of that speaker have. He has taken a catholic survey of the subject and has treated it upon the broad ground of statesmanship, and has presented some valuable suggestions. It would be well for the Convention to reflect upon the points submitted, in the spirit in which they have been given. And I trust that the Legislature, will comprehend from the remarks offered by him here to-day, that the question of Canal Reform is seated deeply in the hearts of the people, and that wise action is needed to extricate the canals from the slough into which they have fallen.

Let us look at the viciousness of a system that is founded upon the principle of extorting the largest amount of money from the State for the least work. It is self-stultification in the most stupendous proportions. What would be thought of any other interest or institution, if the Repair Contract system on the canals was applied to its management? Take the Central Railroad for example. Suppose the Board of Directors were to employ other persons outside of their concern, to keep the road in repair, under contracts that have no relation to each other, and were given out in such a way that the measure of profit shall depend entirely upon the extent to which the contractor can succeed in evading the letter and spirit of his engagement, after having, at a public bidding, been able to secure his contract at a lower rate than anybody else would do the work required, or could do it and live! That is the nature of the canal contract system. How long could the road be run? How long before it would be in ruins? How long before the continual "smashing up" of trains would line its sides with the debris of broken cars, engines, freight of every description, and the mangled bodies of beasts, and even of men and women? Under such a system would not the life insurance companies have all the business they could attend to? What would the Central Road be worth, under such a system of management? Why, Mr. President, it would be speedily blotted out of existence, or the directors would hasten to abolish their policy, and substitute common sense for empiricism.

Suppose, again, Mr. Astor should conceive the idea that he could manage his vast estate under this notable contract system, and should enter into engagements with various persons to keep all his houses in repair, after advertising in the newspapers that he would let the job for a period of ten years to the parties who would agree to do it for the least money! What would be the condition of his houses, stores, shops, etc., on this plan, before half this term should expire? Would he be making money, or saving money by it? Would his property be improved? Would his tenants be satisfied and remain? or would they abandon the tumble-down edifices, in which they found themselves, to the vermin which swarm in dirt and filth—concluding that the landlord was insane, and no longer fit to own and manage the property thus going to ruin? Yet this is the case of the State in its repair of the canals. And I only foreshadow the ruin and desolation which impends over our own public works under this system, by the terms in which I speak of what would happen to the Central Railroad or to Mr. Astor's estate, if they were subjected to the same treatment. So it would be in any other case. As well might the Highway Commissioners of the towns let out the repairs of the roads to the lowest bidder; or a farmer the fencing of his lands and the repairs upon his house and barns; or the owner of a factory or shop—as the State.

The fact is, nobody else is so infatuated as to do business on this scale. Individuals and corporations could not, for it would swiftly bring them to bankruptcy. The State alone, under the inspiration of its "assembled wisdom"—the Legislature—adopts the system; for the State alone is rich enough to pay the cost.

It would seem to be a strange necessity to argue such points as these; and there is none, as far as the conviction of the public mind goes. Every intelligent mind in the State knows that the Repair Contract system is a lamentable failure, and persistence in it an unmitigated outrage; that in no respect does it answer the purposes which it was designed to promote. It does not keep the canal in repair; it does not keep up a good and sufficient navigation; it does not improve the people's property, neither does it save the people's money. It requires no argument or reasoning to establish these facts. Everybody knows all about it now. The thousands of persons who labor to find their sustenance on the canals, know it too well. Their life's blood almost has been drawn from them, in the abortive struggle to make the pursuit of business on the canals a paying or honorable employment. How often has it happened in every year for seven years or more past, that the earnings of a whole season have been swept away by a break in the canals, a break, too, occasioned by the neglect or parsimony of a contractor, who feels after he has got his contract in his pocket, that every dollar laid out in strengthening or raising a bank, or putting a new plank into a waste weir, comes out of his own purse. Why, Mr. President, I have witnessed the effect of one of these breaks, with which the boatman has become so familiar in my own city, and I can hardly find language in which to describe its miseries. I have seen a string of forty miles of boats—twenty on each side—detained for weeks by a catastrophe of this sort. Forty miles of boats in a line. Thousands of teams taking their provender without earning it. Thousands of men, women and children thrown upon their own resources, millions of dollars worth of products and merchandise arrested on the way to a market or destination, bankrupting their owners or reducing them to distress; and all because the State, in the exercise of a penny-wise and pound-foolish discretion, has abdicated its power, and shirked its duty in keeping its public works, its grand water communications between the abounding West and the seaboard marts of commerce, in a safe, secure and efficient condition. All the horrors of a break in summer are redoubled by a break occurring near the close of the season, from the effect of heavy autumnal storms. The boats then detained are liable to be laid up for good, and exposed to all the hazards of ice and frosts in situations far more difficult to provide for, than when properly harbored. The property on board is also subject to triple hazards and expense of protection or removal. But perhaps I need not dilate further on this theme.

The mystery in this matter is this: how should a system so fraught with dangers and disasters to the business interests of the people, be so entwined into the administration of the government

—a government, too, that is but the breath of the people—as to be continued from year to year, and be so firmly engrafted upon our public policy as to resist every attempt at its eradication? The public sentiment is against it and calls loudly for its abandonment. From all sorts and conditions of men the strongest language in its condemnation is heard. The boatmen are against it, the forwarding merchants are against it, the press is against it, (though I must add, parenthetically, that the press has failed of doing its whole duty, in respect to so crying an evil,) the principal officers charged with the custody and care of the canals are against it. I refer to the Canal Commissioners and State Engineers, who have repeatedly recommended its abolition in their official reports; the people of the Great West, whose prosperity depends in such a large measure upon the successful working of the canals of this State, have protested against it. What then is the secret of the preservation and continuance of the foul thing?

Mr. President, one of the miseries of our situation, and the grand secret of its continued imposition upon us, is found in the self-sustaining forces of the system itself. It is entrenched in corruption, and survives by corruption. The contract system is so lucrative that the contractors are enabled to maintain their hold upon the canals by the very means which they extort from the Treasury. Canal officials are sometimes the partners in the fraudulent transactions growing out of the workings of the system. Let any intelligent and disinterested man look over the history of the Dorn Impeachment, and say, if he can, that this allegation is not true. Canal contractors are a powerful class in our methods of selecting candidates for public office, and in electing those who can afterwards be used by them. But it is chiefly in the Legislature that the defense and protection of the repair system is most successfully operated. It is there, indeed, where all the corruptions, emanating from this fruitful source, exert their most baleful influence. It is in the province of the Legislature to strike the system out of existence; to annihilate it at a blow. But the Legislature has not done it, and we do not know that it intends to do it. We are here to-day to see what we can do to brace the honest men at the Capitol up to the work of the demolition of this wicked system, and to awe the dishonest ones into retirement from the contest.

Many bills have been introduced into both branches of the Legislature to repeal the Contract Law; but if they passed one House, they have been defeated in the other, by means only known to those most familiar with the tricks and expedients which disgrace legislation. In the issue tried between the People of the State and the Contractors, the People have been beaten, and their interests have been sacrificed.

So often have the efforts to change the policy of the State in this respect been baffled, that reform is almost despaired of by the best minds in the State. It was out of the corruption generated upon the canals, and extending into such numerous ramifications that the idea of selling the public property in, and control over, these works arose. Public sentiment does not favor this alternative as a remedy. What course is left to us? Is there any other but that of combining our efforts in a resolute, unflinching determination to clear out this modern Augean stable, and expel the parasites, who fatten upon the robbery of the State, from their strongholds?

It can be done, and must be done. Let the business men of the State join, shoulder to shoulder, and put their shoulders to the wheel, and the great cause of the People against the rotten system that is draining the Treasury, ruining our finances, making heavy and grievous the burdens of taxation, undermining the morals of society, and even endangering Republican institutions, must and shall triumph. Let the harpies understand this, and get ready to set their houses in order, and give back to the People what they have wrested, and now wrongfully withhold, from them.

I cannot close my remarks—more extended than I had wished—without alluding to the position recently assumed by the Auditor in his Annual Report. That officer has strangely enough found it within the line of his duty to defend the present system. He referred to an example on the Champlain Canal, in which it had cost a larger sum of money to put a section in a good state of repair than was offered by an individual. This was indeed a most extraordinary illustration of the beauty and virtue of the system. I know something about the Champlain Canal, in the performance of my duty as the Attorney of the State, under Senator Stanford's investigating Committee. I have come by this knowledge, and I know what is my responsibility, when I aver that some of the most infamous instances of dereliction and peculation have been practiced upon the Champlain Canal. Its navigation has been almost ruined. In the particular case cited by the Auditor, where $60,000 had been expended by the State in restoring a section, it was safe to charge that the liability to the expenditure grew out of the remissness of a previous contractor. He had not fulfilled his contract, and the canal of course was going into dilapidation. That is true of all the canals. They are filling up and going to decay, and in ten years more, under the present order of superintendence, the State will have to rebuild them. The monuments of the system would ultimately be a rich body of contractors, a depleted treasury, and the public works in ruins.

In proposing to abolish the existing system it might be asked, before we did so, what we would substitute for it. We cannot go on with things in a worse condition than they are. So fatally damaging is the present system to the best interests of the

State, that we should lose no time in sweeping it from the Statute-book. We should make thorough work of it, too, striking down the system and vacating existing contracts together. Let the whole pollution perish at once. I have no doubt that a method could be devised for executing these repairs that would be safe, economical and efficient. The percentages now bestowed in the corruption of officials and members of the Legislature could at least be saved. The State of New-York—the great State of New-York, the Empire State, par excellence—would be saved the pitiable spectacle of being robbed in its exchequer for the purpose of corrupting its public functionaries, and of paying more for an inefficient system of canal navigation than it should cost to keep it in the best condition.

I will conclude by expressing the hope that this Convention will unite in the unanimous and emphatic adoption of the resolutions, and the Committee appointed by the Convention shall go to Albany and demand the repeal of the contract system. The people will be satisfied with nothing less than its entire abrogation.

SPEECH OF CHARLES A. KING, Esq., OF TOLEDO.

Mr. President and Gentlemen:

We come from Toledo, a lake-shore city, which is identified with you in the trade of the Lakes, and the Erie Canal as a continuation of the Lakes, and which makes the trade of the Lakes valuable. We do not come to interfere with your local affairs, nor with the management of your canals; but we do come to you alarmed for our interests and prosperity, in view of the diversion of trade from our lakes and from you, and we desire to point out the drift of trade to your and our own prejudice. Let us, therefore, reason together as to our tendencies, and consult together as to our best interests, which require cheap transportation, in order to preserve our prominence as lake-shore cities, and to protect the commerce of the Empire State.

We both, twelve years ago, enjoyed the trade which then sustained a daily line of propellers from Buffalo to Cleveland; a daily line of propellers from Buffalo to Sandusky, and twice the number of propellers from Buffalo to Toledo, our city, that is now employed in our trade; and twice the number of propellers between Buffalo and Detroit that are now employed, and then these propellers were sustained and run in connection with the Erie Canal. Now, how is it? Not a propeller on the Lakes is running in connection with lines on the Erie Canal; but a few are running in connection with and in the interest of railroad lines. Some of them, it is true, run in connection with railroads of the State of New-York, and some of them in the interest of a Philadelphia railroad from Erie.

Let us, therefore, look this thing square in the face, and see how our trade is diverted, and the effect of that diversion upon your and our interests. We recognize three rival cities on the Atlantic coast, New-York, Philadelphia and Baltimore, all anxious to secure the valuable trade of the West. And what are the efforts put forth to secure that trade? You know, of your own. Let us see what Philadelphia is doing. Philadelphia sends out a double-track railroad, across the mountains to Pittsburg, and by the Pittsburg, Fort Wayne & Chicago Railroad runs a line within fifty miles south of Lake Erie and parallel with it east and west, converging to Chicago on the south end of Lake Michigan. And not satisfied with that, they send another branch from Pittsburg, by the Pan-Handle route, fifty miles south of and parallel with the Pittsburg, Fort Wayne and Chicago Road, and extending west to Peoria, passing only fifty miles south of Lake Michigan, thereby cutting off Chicago from your trade. They are doing even more to divert your trade, as Philadelphia sends out the Philadelphia and Erie Railroad to Erie, and by a line of propellers and the Empire line of cars, is competing for the trade of the Lakes, and the northern lines of railroads, for our trade, at a discrimination of five cents per 100 lbs., in favor of Philadelphia, over the lowest rates through your State to New-York, and at the same rates through Pennsylvania and New Jersey as are paid through your State to your Empire City; thereby depriving New-York State of the benefit of the transportation, as well as New-York City of the trade. Philadelphia does not stop at that, but runs a road to our Lakes, at Cleveland, known as the Cleveland and Pittsburg Railroad, to further control trade from our Lakes and from you.

Added to all this, Philadelphia is building and has built warehouses, and stores grain seven days for three-tenths of one cent per bushel, and thirty days for one cent per bushel. We have thus glanced at the reaching out of Philadelphia: let us review the efforts of Baltimore to control the trade which has heretofore flowed without interruption to your State for transportation, and to your city for a market. Baltimore sends out a road to Wheeling, and by lease or purchase connects with the Cincinnati & Marietta Railroad, running east and west some eighty miles south of the southern line out by Philadelphia, by the Pan-Handle route from Pittsburg. And, not satisfied to leave us a strip of country eighty miles wide for our trade, they run lines north to Dayton, about half way between the southern line from Philadelphia, and thence east and west; thereby, with Philadelphia, running four lines behind us, respectively about forty and fifty miles apart, thereby draining the trade of the country for twenty or twenty-five miles on either hand of such lines of railroad to Philadelphia or Baltimore, to the prejudice of our Lakes, the injury of the Erie Canal and the State of New-York, and the loss of trade to the City of New-York. In fact leaving, without rivals, a strip of country only forty miles wide, south of the Lakes, to sustain the great trade of the Lakes and the Erie Canal.

Gentlemen, we do not come to you and ask you to consider these things, and help us to meet this competition, without first having ourselves done all we could do to preserve our trade. Our canals and railroads have been built as tributaries to the Lakes and Erie Canal, and we have reduced our tolls to meet competition; and to-day the tolls on the Ohio Canal are three cents per bushel on wheat, and eight cents per barrel on flour, for three hundred and ten miles; whereas the Erie Canal charges six cents and a fraction tolls on wheat, and twenty-two and three-tenths per barrel on flour, for three hundred and sixty miles, or about one hundred per cent. on wheat and one hundred and seventy-five per cent. on flour higher than on our canals, which were built as feeders to you, and which depend on you for success. As to our railroads, we can only refer you to the value of the stock, respectively, of the Cleveland, Columbus & Cincinnati Road, the Sandusky, Mansfield & Newark Railroad, the Sandusky & Cincinnati Railroad, the Dayton & Michigan, and the Toledo, Wabash & Western Railroad, acknowledged as railroads built to be feeders to your and our trade. Some of them are worthless stock, and the best are working without sufficient remuneration to make their stock near par to control the small trade of the West, relatively, which you still retain.

Gentlemen, we have thus tried to present to you your own and our interests, which are indentical. We will not attempt to show you how the trade of Chicago is controlled by the Mississippi River, but we know that St. Louis is drawing away for the Mississippi, as we at Toledo compete with Chicago and St. Louis for the same trade, south of Chicago; and we know whereof we speak, when we say that the Mississippi route is drawing away from us, Chicago and you; but we will say that, in the trade of Chicago, you have other rivals, as we have watched the trade and find that four trunk lines converge at Chicago, namely: the Michigan Central, the Michigan Southern, the Pittsburg, Fort Wayne & Chicago, and the Great Eastern line.

The first, it is true, is tributary to your New-York Central Railroad, and the Grand Trunk; the second, to your Central Erie, and Erie and Philadelphia Railroad, the two securing a portion to your State for transportation to New England and your Empire City; but the third, the Pittsburg, Fort Wayne and Chicago, is in the Philadelphia interest; and the fourth, the Great Eastern, is in the Baltimore interest, and all four lines get a fair share of business, or cut to equalize the amount of traffic. At the best you get but half; Philadelphia one-quarter, and Baltimore one-quarter of the whole amount moved by railroad.

But, gentlemen, you have other competition for the trade of the Lakes during the season of navigation. Montreal is reaching out. Without having statistics of Chicago trade, we can only point you to the marine lists of the shipments of Chicago in July, when the clearances of vessels with wheat were to Kingston as a rule, and with corn and oats to Buffalo. But of our trade, we can say that of the 7,500,000 bushels of wheat received by Toledo after the harvest of 1869, 2,000,000 bushels went to Montreal, and more would have gone to Liverpool by that route if facilities had been obtained. And why? Simply from the fact that they gave us cheaper facilities. Let us compare the cost of transportation through you to Liverpool, and *via* Montreal, on a bushel of wheat:

	Cents.
Toledo to Buffalo	4
At Buffalo	2
Erie Canal	14
Ocean freights, New-York to Liverpool (10¼d. sterling)	26½—46½

Toledo to Kingston	7½
Kingston to Montreal	5
Montreal to Liverpool (12d. sterling)	30 —42½

Hence you see that, calling the insurance and transferring to ship the same in New-York as in Montreal, that Montreal has an advantage over your route of four cents per bushel on wheat to Liverpool, the great and controlling market for our agricultural products. And, gentlemen, what is four cents per bushel to the West? I will not attempt to compute it, but from careful estimates we at Toledo can say, that we have an area of country and development now fully 2,000,000 acres cultivated in wheat, 3,000,000 acres cultivated in corn, and 1,000,000 acres cultivated in oats, tributary to Toledo, producing respectively fifteen bushels of wheat to the acre, and a saving of four cents per bushel is 60 cents per acre, or $1,200,000 ; on corn, 40 bushels to the acre is 160 cents per acre, or $4,800,000 ; and on oats, 40 bushels to the acre of half the weight is 80 cents per acre, or $800,000—or a grand total of $6,800,000 per annum.

I do not claim that all this property seeks transportation; but I do claim that its value to the producer is just what it is worth to ship, and that our agriculturists realize the full limit of my estimate by the small saving of four cents per bushel in grain freights.

Gentlemen, I have thus attempted to show you the efforts made by your rivals to draw trade from the Lakes, you and ourselves, and also our efforts to hold our trade and the cheaper route to the markets of the Old World—all affecting you and drawing off your trade, and all, except the Montreal route, hurting the lake cities and destroying the trade of the Lakes.

Gentlemen, it is for you to say, whether you will meet our efforts to protect you and ourselves, our lake cities and our lake interests, by cheap, reliable and speedy transportation on the Erie Canal.

After other addresses in favor of the Resolutions, as reported, and condemning the present condition of the canals and the contract system,

The question of the adoption of the Resolutions was put to the Convention by the President, and THE RESOLUTIONS AS REPORTED WERE UNANIMOUSLY ADOPTED.

(*See Resolutions, pages* 42 *and* 43.)

The following Resolutions were then offered, and unanimously adopted by the Convention, viz. :

Resolution offered by M. M. CALEB, Esq.

Resolved, That our Senators and Representatives in Congress be requested to use their influence to repeal the Act imposing tonnage dues on Canal Boats.

Resolution offered by L. J. N. STARK, Esq.

Resolved, That the Board of Canal Appraisers should be abolished, and a Court of Claims, with full judicial powers, should be created in its stead, with three judges at adequate salaries.

Resolutions offered by FRANCIS D. MOULTON, Esq.

Resolved, That the thanks of this Convention be tendered to the Mayor and Common Council of the City of Rochester, for the courteous reception given by them to the Commercial Union, and for their attendance at this Convention.

To which Resolution, Mayor Smith, of Rochester, responded.

Resolved, That the thanks of this Convention be tendered to the Hon. Henry L. Fish, ex-Mayor of Rochester, for the attention shown to the visitors and delegates to this Convention.

Resolution offered by MR. THURSTON :

Resolved, That the thanks of the Convention are due and are hereby tendered to the Press of the State of New-York, for their efforts in behalf of the present movement for the reform of the canal management and trade.

Resolution offered by HON. ISRAEL T. HATCH:

Resolved, That the thanks of this Convention are due and are hereby tendered to the President of the Commercial Convention, Nathaniel Sands, Esq., for the able manner in which he has presided over the deliberations of the Convention.

The President, Mr. SANDS, in response to the resolution of thanks, addressed the Convention.

CLOSING REMARKS OF MR. SANDS.

I beg leave to return thanks to the Convention for the resolution they have just passed, and to say a few parting words. One of the greatest needs of the day is the reduction of the Canal Tolls. We must make the Erie Canal the cheapest route of transportation in the State, and so attract all the coarser freight which must have inexpensive carriage from the Western States to the sea. The Canal Board, with the concurrence of the Legislature, has the power to reduce the tolls to any figure they please, even if the revenues on such reduction do not suffice to pay the debts provided for in the Constitution. The deficit can be raised by tax if need be. But I prefer the plan advocated by the gentleman from Buffalo (Mr. Hatch). He proposes to fund the balance of the canal debt and extend its payment over eighteen years. This will relieve our people from a direct tax and enable us to so reduce the tolls as to obtain virtually a free canal. I approve of the project of funding the debt. It is not true that we are thus postponing the evil day of payment. We are simply placing on posterity a part of the burdens, which must be borne in order to make posterity wealthy. In eighteen years from now, when the last dollar of the debt is paid, our State will be so rich through a free canal, that it will not feel the burden of payment. Therefore I favor the funding measure, and we must demand from the Legislature and the Canal Board: 1, Reduction of Tolls; 2, Funding of the balance of the Canal Debt. We are about to return again to our homes and our daily avocations. But let us not forget the work that we have so successfully begun, for its importance cannot be over-estimated in its bearings upon the prosperity of the State at large and hundreds of thousands of its inhabitants. Gentlemen, great enterprises and undertakings are only accomplished through labor and patient application, equal in all respects to the magnitude of the ends sought to be attained. Forward, then, to our *Work*. Let us march on to victory. The Commercial Union will soon number 50,000 members, and before a year rolls round to celebrate the anniversary of this Convention, I trust it will be a hundred thousand strong, composed of all those men whose labor and whose intellect have built up so many beautiful towns and cities, like the one we are now assembled in, along the banks of the great canals of the State. We can then go to the Legislature, not as supplicants, not as beggars humbly praying for a few crumbs of relief, but as sovereigns claiming our rights. The people—the people will go in a solid body, strong and thoroughly organized.

Gentlemen, again thanking you and in saying farewell, my parting words to you are to work!! Work triumphs where words, where eloquence, where genius and all else fail.

The Convention then adjourned *sine die.*

APPENDIX.

PROCEEDINGS of the Common Council of Buffalo, held Tuesday, January 18, 1870, at 2:30 o'clock, P.M., in the Common Council Chamber, in the City of Buffalo.

(From the Buffalo Courier, of January 19, 1870.)

ROCHESTER CANAL CONVENTION.

Ald. Sears, from the Special Committee, offered the following resolution:

The Committee appointed by the Council to act in reference to the Canal Convention to be held at Rochester, on the 19th inst., respectfully report the following:

The City of Buffalo is largely interested in the prosperity, good management, and proper government of the Erie Canal in common with the whole State of New-York.

And Whereas, by reason of the contract system and other causes the canal is and has been unable to carry property expeditiously, and with safety, the high rates of tolls have diverted traffic, and the State of New-York and the City of Buffalo, in particular, have suffered through diversion of business and a reduction of receipts;

And Whereas, a Convention has been called to be held at Rochester on the 19th inst., to take into consideration these evils, and devise some means to remedy them: Therefore, be it

Resolved, 1st, That this Council recommend the abolishment of the contract system.

2d, A proper reduction of tolls.

3d, That the Erie Canal be fully completed according to the plan of enlargement thereof; that is, seven feet deep, seventy feet broad, fifty-four feet broad at bottom; old bench walls removed and double locks throughout the entire length.

Resolved, That this Council attend the said Convention and urge the adoption of the above preamble and resolutions, or similar ones. And that this Council do appropriate the sum of $300, or as much thereof as may be necessary, to defray the expenses of this Council in attending said Convention, and direct the Treasurer to pay the same to the chairman of this committee.

The report was adopted, with the resolutions.

RECEPTION

By the Mayor and Common Council of the City of Rochester, of the Central Committee of the Commercial Union, on arriving at Rochester.

(From the Rochester Democrat, of January 18, 1870.)

ARRIVAL OF DELEGATES FOR THE CANAL CONVENTION.

On the 10:20 train from the East last evening, Nathaniel Sands, President, Joseph F. Daly, Secretary, L. J. N. Stark and M. M. Caleb of the State Central Committee of the Commercial Union, and delegates to the Convention from New-York to be held tomorrow, arrived, and were taken to the Osburn House, where they were met by Mayor Smith, Ex-Mayor Fish, several Aldermen and representatives of the Press. Mayor Smith, in a few well chosen words, welcomed the gentlemen and tendered to them the hospitality of the city. A public reception, he stated, would have been given them had it not been understood that it would not have been acceptable.

Mr. Sands, in behalf of the delegation, said that he appreciated the kindness of the citizens of Rochester in tendering their hospitality. They were all business men, and they knew that the purpose of their present visit was work. He had before visited Rochester, and regarded it as a very thriving city, and took pleasure in looking at the many evidences of prosperity which it exhibited. When the call was made for the Convention to meet in this city, he considered that no more appropriate place could have been chosen.

At the suggestion of Mayor Smith, Mr. Sands stated in brief as follows, the object of the present Convention.

First—To effect a change through the Legislature in the organic law respecting the management of the canals.

Second—The reduction of canal tolls, so as to make the canal the great water highway of the State for transportation.

Third—To make transportation speedy, as well as certain. Canal men regard breaks and all delays as unnecessary and avoidable, and they proposed to introduce a system which would remedy every defect of this kind which is now existing.

Ex-Mayor Fish said it was the design of the Convention to hold out inducements to men to invent improved and perfect lock gates, such as can be opened and shut in a moment; also for towing by steam.

Other delegates to the Convention, from New-York, Buffalo, Oswego and other cities arrived this forenoon. This afternoon there will be an informal meeting of the delegates in the parlors of the Osburn House, when a programme of business for the Convention will be made and other necessary business transacted. The session to-morrow forenoon will be occupied doubtless in perfecting an organization.

PROCEEDINGS OF THE NEW-YORK PRODUCE EXCHANGE ON JANUARY 13, 1870.

(*From the New-York Times, January* 14, 1870.)

IMPROVING THE CANALS—IMPORTANT MEETING AT THE PRODUCE EXCHANGE—APPOINTMENT OF A DELEGATION TO THE COMMERCIAL UNION CONVENTION, AT ROCHESTER.

A meeting was held at the Produce Exchange, at 1 o'clock P. M., yesterday, to take into consideration the propriety of sending delegates to represent the produce dealers of this city at a Convention of the Commercial Union of the State of New-York, to be held at Rochester, on Wednesday next. The object of this Convention is to set on foot measures to increase the facilities for improving the navigation of the Erie Canal and its tributaries. The meeting was called to order by Mr. S. D. Harrison, President of the Produce Exchange. Mr. Carlos Cobb was elected Chairman, who, on assuming the duties of presiding officer, said that from time to time, heretofore, attempts had been made in public meetings of this character to set on foot measures having this result, but as yet the desideratum was not attained. Now a new feeling had arisen with regard to it, and there had been formed a Commercial Union for the purpose of devising means whereby the relief long sought for might be secured. He was proud to say that this Union or Association had its origin in this city, and was participated in by men of influence and energy, a fact which augured well for the final success of the organization. This Association, however, was not confined to the City of New-York. It had members over the whole State, and especially among the owners of property all along the line of the Erie Canal and its tributaries, and embraced men of the greatest influence. He was glad to see that the Committee of the Legislature named in connection with the canal interests of New-York was composed of men favorable to intelligent action on the matter of increased facilities for navigation. He was glad to know, too, that the Produce Exchange was taking an interest in the subject. It had been a stigma, heretofore, that a lukewarmness had prevailed in relation to this question. People had supposed that because produce had heretofore been brought to this city by means of the canal, that, therefore, it would continue to come in sufficient quantities to satisfy all demands. Now, our best men are thinking on this subject, and were determined to provide for an increase of facilities for supplying this market. It was well known that there were rival lines of transportation disputing this traffic with New-York; and many persons set too little importance on it. What would have been the value of a vast deal of property here to-day but for this very traffic? The trade of the Canal and its tributaries had done more than probably any other thing to increase property values in this metropolis. The question was now to be agitated, how shall the means for this traffic be increased; or, at least, what measures are necessary to prevent the facilities for carrying on this trade from becoming less than they now are? A Convention to discuss this important matter will be held in Rochester, on Wednesday, the 19th instant, and it is desirable that a delegation should go from this city to represent the interests of the produce dealers of New-York in that Convention.

Mr. J. Hobart Herrick was then elected Secretary of the meeting.

Colonel Edward Hincken then offered the following resolutions, which were unanimously adopted:

Whereas, The members of the Produce Exchange recognize the necessity of reforming the official management and improving the trade of the canals of the State of New-York; therefore,

Resolved, That the Commercial Union, which has been ably organized to secure these ends, deserves and shall receive our utmost aid and influence.

Resolved, That a committee of forty from the Produce Exchange be appointed to attend the Convention of the Commercial Union, to be held in Rochester, on Wednesday, January 19, at 10 o'clock A. M.

The Chair appointed, as delegates under the above resolution, the following gentlemen:

S. D. Harrison, Jesse Hoyt, L. Hazeltine, David Dows, Alex. E. Orr, J. M. Fiske, Arthur Fiske, J. H. Herrick, Adon Smith, E. W. Coleman, C. Parish, Carlos Cobb, S. K. Lane, E. S. Brown, A. E. Masters, L. B. Shaw, R. H. Laimbeer, W. B. Barber, Henry Buell, U. C. Whitlock, E. H. Tompkins, M. M. Caleb, A. R. Gray, B. P. Baker, L. J. N. Stark, Archibald Baxter, William H. Power, Benjamin Logan, A. F. Roberts, G. D. Cragin, Robert P. Getty, J. S. Williams, R. B. Minturn, C. H. Marshall, G. A. Brett, Edward Hincken, J. W. Elwell, J. M. Boynton, E. Annann, George D. Puffer, Geo. W. Smith, A. S. Jewell, F. Edson, Milton Knapp, J. P. Wallis.

The Chairman was added to the Committee, and the meeting, after giving three cheers for the Commercial Union, adjourned.

CANAL TOLLS.

REVISION OF RATES OF CANAL TOLLS—ARGUMENT OF MR. H. NILES, BEFORE THE CANAL BOARD AT ALBANY, N. Y.

Mr. President and Gentlemen of the Canal Board:

It may not be impertinent to the subject in regard to which this delegation has appeared before you, to preface whatever I have to present or urge in favor of a revision of the present toll list, with the assurance that our mission here is not for the advancement of any private or personal interest of ours, nor for the promotion of any sectional or local interest of those who delegated us. On the contrary, we have come here from the extreme and central parts of the State, representing all classes of trade, manufactures and commerce, in behalf of the great interests of the State, as connected with her noble system of public works, deeply impressed with the truth that a radical reform in the management and care of the canals is absolutely necessary, and immediately required, to protect and bear them forward to the fulfilment of the great destiny for which they were so wisely conceived and created.

In presenting before your honorable body some propositions and practical suggestions upon the subject of a revision of the present sheet and rates of tolls, I offer them as the results of and conclusions drawn from personal observation and long experience in commercial pursuits, more especially in the carrying trade upon the canals of our State. Perhaps I may not more happily introduce the subject than by quoting an extract from the memorial of the State Canal Convention (held in this city one year since), in which, upon the subject of "a revision of the rates of toll," it was said :

"Your memorialists and others most fully concur in a remark upon this subject in the last report of the canal department. "The rates of toll," says the document, "should be adjusted and distributed upon property intended for transit on the canals, so as to *retain* the trade and *prevent* diversion." There is a volume of wisdom in this assertion which should command immediate attention from the Legislature and Canal Board. Do we not all know that some of the most important articles of traffic are now almost wholly withdrawn from the canals, owing to the rivalry of railroads ? While we would sacredly uphold the constitutional guarantees connected with the tolls for paying the public creditors for our canal debt, we would respectfully suggest that the concurrent action of the Legislature and Canal Board might be made to increase the revenue by reducing the tolls on articles which are now almost wholly excluded from canal traffic. Large quantities of freight might thus be brought back to canals, from which comparatively little is now derived. Thorough revision of the toll list is, therefore, respectfully recommended for this purpose, in reference to several ponderous articles, some reduction on which would probably considerably enlarge the canal revenue, while enabling the forwarders and boatmen to rely always on freight from the seaboard to the interior. It needs no argument to prove that, if there is always freight enough to go West, the forwarders can work more profitably for the public and themselves than if they had to rely chiefly on their own down freights to pay the expenses of vessels that have often to go Westward without cargoes. Besides all this, forwarders would be able to bring Western produce more cheaply to the seaboard, if reliance could always be made on having sufficient freight to pay their expenses in returning Westward.

The interest of the western producers and the eastern consumers are thus concerned in requiring a prompt revision of the toll-sheet, so as to enable the canals to compete with railroads, by getting back at least a portion of trade that is driven from them by high toll.

My first proposition is, that under the original policy adopted in our canal system, private enterprise and private capital were invited to furnish, equip and operate the canals; therefore, that large industrial class of our citizens who have responded and invested their capital, and made this their avocation, are so immediately connected with the canal interests of the State that their business and means are alike dependent upon a wise administration of canal affairs, whether it be in the substantial care and supervision of the canals, or in a wise adjustment of tolls. Hence the relative position this interest occupies toward the State, with respect to the canals, is second only to that of the State, and paramount as regards all others.

The second proposition is, that the interests of the State and of the carrier are identical in promoting and bringing to the canals the greatest amount of traffic, consistent with the greatest amount of revenue that it is possible for them to sustain without repelling commerce and diverting trade.

The third proposition I have to offer is—that the toll-sheet established by this department is to the canals of the State, what the freight tariffs are to the railroads, and must necessarily exercise some relative bearing and effect, either for good or evil, in promoting the welfare of the State.

Starting with these propositions, and giving them whatever consideration they are entitled to, I respectfully submit that no one subject or branch of subject which comes under the canal department is of more vital importance, or requires more constant vigilance and study, or perhaps receives less practical attention and consideration, than that of adjusting tolls. If, as has hitherto been generally conceded, water communication furnishes superior facilities in supplying the necessities of commerce, it must also be conceded that under wise and prudent and careful management in the repairs and condition of our canals, and a wise and sagacious adjustment of tolls, our great system of public works will command the preference in the movement of every class of property, which forms its nature, value or locality, is not especially adapted to the speedier movement by rail. If this be true, what must be inferred from the fact, and how can we account for it, that very many, and some of the most important, articles of commerce and traffic are now almost wholly withdrawn from the canals, by diversion to railroads and other channels affording surer facilities and cheaper transit? What, I ask, is to be inferred from this state of facts? Either that water has not the conceded superiority over rail, and consequently our canal system, falsely founded, must yield to its rival the preëminence it has so long retained; or the fault lies in the administration and management of the canals. To this last cause I would prefer to ascribe it, and, if possible, also, I will attempt to discover where the fault lies, rather than tacitly accept the conclusion that the canal system of the Empire State, which emanated from her greatest and wisest statesmen, was a mistake.

We have only to refer to the reports of this department for a series of years to astonish ourselves by noticing the entire extinction of revenue and tonnage, from numerous articles of commerce and trade, which in the aggregate, but a short time since, made up an important item in the annual amount of tolls received and tons carried; and we find many other and important articles following in the same direction. You will find this particularly observable in articles of vegetable food, and all other agricultural products of our own and the Northwestern States going towards tidewater; also, in articles of general merchandise, and various other articles classed under other heads, as manufactures, etc. Your attention will also be drawn to the fact that the greatest apparent diversion is found in the articles charged with the highest rates of toll, which is a significant point in a review or criticism of the present sheet of toll which lies upon your table, and of which we ask a general revision.

If the theory be correct that the management of public affairs, such as those pertaining to our public works, may judiciously be modelled, as nearly as possible, upon the management of a sagacious and successful rival—whether a private individual, or incorporated or joint stock company—this canal toll-sheet might be regarded as an interesting subject for criticism by a practical adept in the freighting department of a well-managed railroad company. Its equivocal classification and inexplicable distribution of rates would certainly excite the wonder of an intelligent mind to conceive the policy which dictated such an adjustment. We find that the original tariff of tolls was evidently based upon the principle that the rate of toll should bear some relative proportion to the value of the article transported. This was both expedient and wise in that early day, as the greater the value of the article the better could it afford the higher toll. There were no rival competing channels or other elements existing at the time to conflict with this policy, which prevailed for years, and the toll-sheet was only changed in its enumeration of the new and various articles of traffic which science and the inventive genius of our country were annually developing. It was not until the influence of improvements in steam upon the Western rivers, and the rivalry of canals in other States began to be realized, that the Canal Board saw the necessity of a reduction in toll, in order to retain the traffic of southern Ohio, Kentucky and Tennessee. To accomplish this object and not impair the revenue, they adopted a discriminating policy, by a reduction of tolls upon certain productions of, and upon merchandise, &c., going to that section, south of a particular point of latitude in the State of Ohio. Thus a precedent was established, and, if we admit the wisdom of the policy of that date of cheapening toll, to retain and increase the traffic, would it be less wise now, the railroad system having in the meantime so developed as to revolutionize the whole internal commerce and transit of the country?

But to return to the toll-sheet. It will be seen at a glance that the principle which dictated the original tariff of tolls and was most wise in that day, is far from being so now. Yet, for the last quarter of a century, during which time this great revolution has been taking place in the internal transit of the country, no general revision has been attempted to be made to meet the necessities growing out of these radical changes. The toll-sheet of to-day is virtually a stereotyped edition of what it was thirty years since, during which time we have witnessed the exodus of half the enumerated articles, in whole or in part, from the canals, and their diversion to the railroads and other channels. It is true that some changes of toll have been made upon articles here and there, and from time to time, but not upon any settled policy which should govern a general revision; and it may be ascribed to this mode of change, instead of such general system of revision, as is now recommended, that this present toll-sheet presents itself to us with all its incongruities.

To attempt a full exposition of these incongruities would be too tedious and would occupy too much of your time. In presenting a single illustration, which will apply with equal force to most other articles constituting the upward or westward bound tonnage, I will cite your attention to the article of iron in its various phases, from the ore to its most highly finished form of cutlery. The following table taken from the toll-sheet before you, I think will present such a bundle of inconsistencies in the distribution of toll that, if the same defects should be found running through the toll-sheet, the general revision suggested may not seem unnecessary.

	Rate of Toll per 1000 lbs. per mile.	Toll per ton from Albany to Buffalo.
No. 4—Iron Ore.............................	1 mill.	70 cents.
No. 9—Iron, old scrap and broken castings........ This is of least value per ton.	2 "	1 40 "
No. 9—Iron, bloom and pig, bolts, iron safes, plow castings, bed plates for steam engines...	2 "	1 40 "
No. 13—Iron, stoves and all other castings, except machines and parts thereof.............	3 "	2 10 "
No. 56—Iron, in bars, bundles, sheets, boiler, bridge, railings, steel nails, spikes, horse-shoes, gas and water pipes, railroad chairs....	1 5 "	1 05 "
No. 58—Iron, railroad iron	2 "	1 40 "
No. 59—Iron, car axles and car wheels.............	2 "	1 40 "
No. 61—Iron, all other articles not enumerated or excepted, going toward tidewater.......	3 "	2 10 "
No. 62—Iron, all other articles not enumerated, going from tidewater........................	1-5 "	1 05 "

From a needle to an anvil, or from a lancet to a trip-hammer, pays the lowest rate of toll.

One would suppose, by finding the products of iron brought under so many different classes or numbers of the toll-sheet of this department, that deep thought and great ability had been bestowed to perfect such a distribution of toll, as would secure to the canals both the traffic and revenue from so important an article of upward tonnage. But, on the contrary, a moment's attention, practically bestowed upon such an adjustment of tolls as this, would surprise almost any one with its inconsistencies, without a word being said to him in exposition of its damaging effects upon the traffic and revenue of the canals, in consequence of rates having been held stereotyped upon the toll-sheet for over thirty years. He might well ask : " Why tax scrap iron and broken castings more than the highest and most perfectly wrought articles of iron and steel manufacture ?" The same would apply to pig and bloom iron, which are the products in its first stage from the furnace and the forge, gross in quality and ponderous in quantity. The same also applies to railroad iron.

Still more inexplicable is the excessive toll of three mills upon the articles of "all other castings" than stoves, "excepting machines and parts thereof," which includes all the heavy castings required for buildings wholly or in part of iron, and for all other structures, and general uses to which it has become so essential at the present day. Why, it may be asked, should these coarse and heavy castings be taxed fifty per cent. more than bed-plates for steam engines, and 10) per cent. more than gas and water pipe? And again, it may, with greater pertinency, be asked, why should all these cheap and ponderous articles of iron enumerated under

Nos. 9, 13, 58 and 59 of the toll-sheet be tolled $33\frac{1}{2}$ per cent. more than the more highly wrought articles enumerated in No. 56, and the most highly finished articles not enumerated? [See No. 59 of toll-sheet.] It would stagger the Auditor of this department, I think, to satisfactorily reconcile these incongruities. He possibly would say the denominations included in Nos. 56 and 59 had been reduced in 1858, and again in 1864, under the denomination of merchandise; but this does not remove, but on the contrary it more fully establishes, the incongruity. If policy dictated a reduction upon the articles of iron embraced in Nos. 56 and 59 to protect the traffic from the diversions, why were it not at least as politic to have extended the reduction to the cheaper and more ponderous articles of iron, which aggregate twenty fold the amount of tonnage, and upon which the present rate of toll amounts to almost a total prohibition, so that the carrier is deprived of the freight, and the State, of the toll?

I will cite a fact illustrative of this result. Last spring several thousand tons of castings were required by Mr. Burch, of Chicago, from tide, upon the Hudson River, to rebuild his extensive block of iron stores then recently burned. By canal, the transportation, including expense of loading and discharging cargo at Buffalo, could be afforded (in fact was offered) at two dollars per ton over toll, which from Albany to Buffalo is two dollars and ten cents; therefore, it would cost four dollars and ten cents per ton. The New-York and Erie Railway could afford to take it at twenty shillings per ton for return freight for their platform and cattle cars, rather than run them up light, it paying them twenty-five dollars per car. Is not this prohibition? The railway competitor, were this adjustment left to him, could scarcely better adjust the toll upon the article of iron to his own advantage. The same will be found true, to a greater or less extent, of a majority of articles constituting the upward bound tonnage, the importance of which to the carrier, and consequently to the State, is doubly enhanced from the fact that the downward tonnage so largely preponderates. More than half the eastern bound boats are compelled to return empty, thus throwing the whole expense of the round trip entirely upon the down freight, which would necessarily be cheapened by even a partial return freight; and, therefore, should the revenue not be materially increased or affected by a protective reduction of toll upon the up tonnage, the benefit would be secured from the increase in the downward movement, incited by the lesser price of freight, which such a change in the present economy of canal transit would induce. This theory should not be lost sight of, as it is for this up tonnage that we meet the strongest competition of the railroads, which may be particularly noticed in the disparity of their rates as between their five several classes; the price of the first class exceeding by 300 per cent. that of their fifth special class.

The subject of a general revision of toll is of so much importance, in a practical sense, and affects so closely both the revenue and commerce of the canals, that it becomes almost inexhaustible. Leaving the matter of the upward movement of tonnage to be referred to again hereafter, I will now direct your attention to the downward movement, as affected by the same causes, to wit: the inconsistent and prohibitive rates of toll. I ask your notice particularly to the article of flour, as a fair representative of every article of "package and rolling freight," derived from the agricultural products of this and the Western States. With regard to all this class of eastward bound tonnage—from which the canal formerly derived an important item of revenue and traffic—no more potent argument can be adduced to show that it has been actually driven from the canals, than a reference to the Auditor's report of trade and tonnage for 1867 (the last report published). In statement 26, folios 256–7, he gives the total quantity of flour arriving at tidewater for a series of years, in giving which, in the briefest and most comprehensive manner, will only give the reports of one year in ten for the last thirty years, as follows:

The number of barrels of flour delivered at tidewater by canal in 1847 was 3,952,072; in 1857, 835,546; and in 1867, 450,050. Of this latter quantity only 15,468 barrels were shipped from Buffalo, the balance, 434,582, being from Oswego, Lockport, Rochester and other points in this State, where the effect of excessive toll is somewhat neutralized by the shorter distance, while the local way freight by rail being higher in proportion to the distance transported, enables the canal to compete and carry some portion of the flour product. This fact is worthy of note, in sustaining the position taken that the excessive toll of 3 mills, or 22.81 cents per barrel from Buffalo to Albany, is prohibitory, and drives this article from the canal. If this is not convincing, I will give an extract from the statistics of the trade and commerce of Buffalo, showing the imports of flour by lake, taken from the United States Custom House, and the exports by canal, taken from the Canal Collector's office, from 1861 to 1868 inclusive.

	Imports by Lake. Barrels.	Exports by Canal. Barrels.
1861	2,159,591	306,236
1862	2,846,022	451,814
1863	2,978,089	469,792
1864	2,028,520	126,820
1865	1,788,393	142,018
1866	1,414,549	52,325
1867	1,417,799	15,468
1868	1,524,818	5,774

It may be added, how could the result be otherwise so long as the freight by rail is 40 cents per barrel to Albany, and the toll by canal within a fraction of 23 cents? The prohibition is too obvious. Why, then, should not the toll be reduced? Surely the State derives no revenue, while the carrier is deprived of the traffic.

I have thus far treated this subject with more particular reference to articles of merchandise, etc., going from the water, and articles of rolling and package freights going toward tidewater, which, from their adaptation to the rail facilities for handling and carrying, have been more especially sought after. And now, since it is discovered that this class of traffic has been almost entirely diverted from the canals, we are awakened to the fact (when too late) that this diversion, to a great extent, might have been prevented by a vigilant watchfulness, and a protective system in the adjustment of tolls. It may now be found difficult to immediately reclaim this lost traffic, but surely this result, from neglect in the past, admonishes us to vigilance in the future. It surely requires neither a seer nor a prophet to predict that, without immediate reform, the entire traffic and tonnage from the agricultural productions of the North-western States, will follow in the train of all this rolling and package traffic, and that, too, at a more rapid rate of diversion than heretofore, as improvements of competing channels and rail facilities progress, with reference to the movement of grain in bulk. Already this is foreshadowed by an analysis of the reports in this department, for which I refer you to Statement No. 16, folio 216, Auditor's Report, 1867:

Tons of Total Movement of Articles on all the Canals from 1861 to 1868 inclusive.

	Product of Forest, tons.	Product of Agriculture, tons.	Product of Manufacture, tons.
1861	1,052,392	2,144,373	280,256
1862	1,569,674	2,494,036	364,887
1863	1,628,688	2,236,075	319,432
1864	1,478,921	1,572,836	282,354
1865	1,467,315	1,696,091	281,832
1866	1,769,994	1,786,060	302,241
1867	1,744,252	1,438,517	320,844
1868	1,958,309	1,442,147	337,262

	Product of Merchandise, Tons.	Product of Other articles, Tons.	Total Tons.
1861	135,096	895,518	4,507,635
1862	167,927	1,002,271	5,598,785
1863	172,278	1,201,219	5,557,692
1864	143,984	1,874,846	4,852,941
1865	154,968	1,129,448	4,729,654
1866	179,878	1,737,047	5,775,220
1867	219,880	1,964,832	5,688,325
1868	324,064	2,344,443	6,442,225

What is most notable in this table is that over ninety per cent. of the total tons moved, falls under three of the above heads, "Forest," "Agriculture," and "Other Articles"—the latter comprises stone, lime, clay, gypsum, coal, copper and iron ores, and sundries—you cannot fail to observe the marked increase of tonnage from the "Forest" and the "mineral products" (other articles), as contrasted with an equally marked decrease or loss of tonnage in the products of agriculture. To render this, if possible, more plain, I compile the following table, showing the relative proportions of tonnage that each of the three classes—"Forest," "Vegetable Food," and "Mineral Products"—bear to the total or aggregate annual movement:

	Total—Tons.	Forest—Tons.	Per cent.
1861	4,507,635	1,052,392	23.34
1862	5,598,785	1,569,674	28.04
1863	5,557,692	1,628,688	29.30
1864	4,852,941	1,478,921	30.47
1865	4,729,654	1,467,315	31.03
1866	5,775,220	1,769,994	30.65
1867	5,688,325	1,744,252	30.67
1868	6,442,225	1,958,309	30 40

	Vegetable Food. Tons.	Per cent.	Other Articles, mostly mineral. Tons.	Per cent.
1861	2,132,237	47 14	895,518	19.88
1862	2,494,036	43.37	1,002,271	17 90
1863	2,236,075	38 58	1,201,219	11.62
1864	1,572,836	31.40	1,374,846	28.33
1865	1,696,091	35.15	1,129,448	13.87
1866	1,786,060	30.54	1,737,047	30.08
1867	1,438,517	34.89	1,964,832	34.54
1868	1,419,175	22.10	2,344,443	35.97

This table speaks volumes, as showing the tendency of traffic. The product of the forest has increased in tonnage, from 1861 to 1868, 905,917 tons, and in its relative proportion of the aggregate movement it has increased 23.34 per cent., in 1861, to 30.40 per cent. in 1868. During the same time, the article of vegetable food has decreased in tonnage 713,062 tons, showing a tonnage of 50 per cent. more in 1861 than in 1868, and in its relative proportion of the aggregate movement it has come down from 47.14 per cent. in 1861 to 22.10 in 1868. Is it not time to seek the cause of this diversion?

It can be nothing less than diversion, for surely the product of vegetable food in the North-western States—for the large and increasing surplus of which those States are demanding new and enlarged channels for its outlet—has not fallen off. The tonnage lost to the canal since 1861, together with the great and boasted increase, does find its outlet to the Atlantic markets by other channels than the Erie Canal, and will continue to so find other and cheaper routes, until this important source of revenue and traffic is entirely diverted to those other routes. We shall then become awake to the fact that this traffic was driven from us by the mistaken policy displayed in the toll-sheet which now lies before you. I come back to my analysis of the table. The increase of the tonnage of "other articles," which are mostly the product of the mines, is remarkable, being 895,518 tons in 1861, and 2,344,443 tons in 1868, an increase of 1,448,925 tons, or about 160 per cent.; and, in relation to the aggregate movement, it has increased from 19.88 per cent. in 1861, to 39.37 per cent. in 1869. The increase under this head is chiefly, if not entirely, attributable to the article of coal, the supply of and demand for which would seem to have no end. A portion of the marked increase of the coal tonnage may be considered fictitious as in comparison to the coal tonnage of 1861, the tons of which westward bound traversed more miles as it was taken up at tidewater. Since 1861 the railroads from the north and west intersecting the canal at Utica, Syracuse, and points at the heads of the Seneca and Cayuga Lakes, have pierced the great coal basins of Pennsylvania, and are laying down coal as cheaply at all the points tributary to the canal as it has heretofore been placed at the delivering points upon the Hudson and the harbor of New-York, at and adjacent to Jersey City. Thus, while this increase represents tons, yet, from the shorter distances these tons are carried upon the canals, neither the traffic nor revenue increased proportionately thereby. But the increase in this traffic, in contrast with that of vegetable food, which has so materially fallen off, contributes to establish the soundness of our theory that it is to the high toll exacted upon vegetable food that its decrease may justly be attributed, for in this, as in all other examples I have given, we find the tonnage of vegetable food languishing and rapidly falling off under the highest rate of toll—three mills—while "other articles," paying one mill and less, are rapidly increasing. But, as regards the article of coal, I am fully persuaded that if the toll should be reduced to half a mill upon the upward tonnage, as it is upon the tonnage going to tidewater, it would be better for the whole interests of the State, as well as the canals, while the revenue would not be prejudiced thereby. First, this would serve to secure the outlet from the mines at tidewater, which would secure its carriage the greater distance upon the canal, as well to the benefit of the carrier as to the revenue. Secondly, as nine-tenths of eastward bound tonnage finds its destination at New-York, it is there that the return coal tonnage is wanted to freight these empty boats, which prefer to take the up-cargo at tidewater, than to risk the uncertainty of a load and questionable prices on arriving at Syracuse, or running up to Ithaca or Havana. Again, the class of boats required to carry barley, oats, malt, flour or other bulky articles, cannot return light, on account of bridges. Consequently they require this coal tonnage at tidewater. The interest of the State and the interest of the carrier harmonize in all the practical economy of transit; and, even in this movement of coal, its retention by the canal depends upon cultivating this harmony.

The New-York and Erie Railroad are carrying large quantities already, both to Buffalo, Dunkirk and Erie. This class of freight is desirable railroad freight, at $2 a ton from Scranton or

South Bend to Buffalo; or at say $20 to $25 per car load, to load back their return cars, particularly their platform and cattle cars.

I have already occupied too much of your time, and will leave it to my colleagues to cover the ground I have not gone over. I regret that in view of the importance of this subject, it is not in my power to do justice to it, or to myself. It is said that "CHEAP TRANSPORTATION IS THE PROBLEM OF STATESMANSHIP AND POWER."

I have one suggestion to make in connection with this subject, if it may not be considered presumptuous. It is, that, to perfect a better system for the wise adjustment of tolls to meet all the exigencies of the times, this department might call to one of its bureaus a practical expert, a man of superior ability, sagacity and experience, in the freighting departments of our most extensive and important channels of commerce, both water and rail. This man should be thoroughly versed in all the elements of internal commerce and transit, familiar with all the rival and competing channels of trade, geographical points, lines and distances; and also versed in the mysteries and power of combinations and through connections in all directions, as well as acquainted with all the sources of traffic. He should have studied, and should understand, the true economy of transportation—the importance of a counter movement when downward movement largely predominates, and, in fine, be an adept, who shall make the subject a speciality and a scientific study.

(*From the N. Y. Tribune, March* 10, 1870.)

FREE CANAL NAVIGATION.

SPEECHES BY THE HON. ELIJAH WARD, MR. F. D. MOULTON, I. T. HATCH, ERASTUS BROOKS, ETC.—LETTERS AND RESOLUTIONS.

The various commercial interests of the city were represented yesterday at the Chamber of Commerce, to confer upon the proper canal policy of this State and the bills on that subject now before the Legislature. Among those present were gentlemen connected with the Commercial Union, Chamber of Commerce, New-York Produce Exchange, Citizens' Association, and Shipowners' Association.

Mr. Peter Cooper occupied the Chair, and briefly informed the meeting that the subject under discussion was free canal navigation, and the advantages following in its train, and called upon Mr. Israel T. Hatch to state more fully the objects of the meeting.

Mr. Hatch proceeded to unfold a plan for rendering the canals free in time by reducing their tolls, which was to be accomplished by a Funding Bill. This Bill is to be introduced at once into the Legislature. It provides for a new loan extending over 18 years, to extinguish the several debts for which the canal revenues are now pledged. This will relieve the canals from this burden, and will leave the Legislature and the Canal Board power to reduce the tolls to a point that will attract the whole freight of the West.

Mr. Joseph F. Daly, Secretary of the Commercial Union, read the following letters from Mr. Wm. M. Evarts and Judge Comstock.

March 3, 1870.
Hon. I. T. Hatch—

DEAR SIR:—I write this note in answer to yours of a recent date asking my opinion as to the constitutionality of a law embracing the following points: 1. The funding of the Canal Debt at eighteen years' time. 2. The appropriation of the canal revenues in part as a sinking fund to pay the debt, proposed to be funded, and in part to the improvement of the canals. 3. The reduction of the tolls.

The Constitution pledges the revenues to pay the existing Canal Debt. While the debt remains, the pledge is in force. But the State has never lost the power of *paying* any part of its debt as soon as it matures. A proposition to fund the Canal Debt at eighteen years, is simply a proposition to borrow money on eighteen years' time, and with it to pay off the creditors who hold the debt.

I suppose that no one will doubt that this is constitutional. The new loan must be contracted according to the 12th section of the Financial article. It must be authorized by an Act of the Legislature and approved by the people. The same Act must specify the object of the loan, and provide for its payment in 18 years by taxation. In this manner and under these limitations, the Constitution has reserved to the Legislature and the people the right to borrow money for any purpose, including the payment of any existing and maturing debt. The Canal Debt being thus provided for, and the new loan being then secured upon the whole property of the people of the State, the liberation of the tolls from the constitutional pledge necessarily follows, and they can be disposed of at the pleasure of the Legislature. They can be used for the improvement of the canals; they can be turned over to a new sinking fund for the payment of the new debt; they can be appropriated to both these purposes. The whole question is one of expediency and not of constitutional law.

As to the reduction of the tolls, the requirement of the Constitution is that they shall not be reduced below the standard of 1852, without the concurrent action of the Canal Board and the Legislature. This requires no comment, because it is plain that the reduction can be made by concurrent action, and cannot in any other manner.

Very respectfully yours,
GEO. F. COMSTOCK.

We have examined the questions considered in the foregoing opinion, and we fully concur in the views and conclusions of Judge Comstock.

March 7, 1870.
JOHN K. PORTER.
JOHN GANSON.

NEW-YORK, *March* 7, 1870.

The Hon. Israel T. Hatch—

MY DEAR SIR: I have considered the subject to which you have called my attention, and which embraces (1) the extinguishing the present Canal Debt of the State by means of a new loan; (2) the application of the canal revenues to the improvement of the canals; and a sinking fund for the redemption of the new loan as the interests of the State may dictate; and (3) the reduction of the canal tolls in promotion of the inland trade, foreign commerce, and general wealth of the State.

There can be no doubt that when the holders of the existing debt of the State, for which the moneys of the canals are pledged by the seventh article of the Constitution, are satisfied, the revenues of the canals will be liberated from the pledge, and the canals, in respect both of the rate of tolls and of the application of their revenues, will be open to such administration as the interests of the people of the State, in the development of population and wealth, and in the promotion of good government, may dictate.

It is equally clear that the satisfaction of the existing debt, by means provided through a new loan, raised in conformity with the twelfth section of the seventh article of the Constitution (which, as is well known, requires the sanction of a direct vote of the people to such new loan), would accomplish the object of relieving the canal revenues from the subsisting pledge as completely, and with as full a maintenance of the rights of the public creditors, as the slower and less certain process of liquidation out of the canal revenues specially provided by the Constitution.

The proposed financial measure of a new loan is wholly free from constitutional objections, adequately meets the rights of the public creditors and the obligations of the State, and relieves the resources of the State for properly dealing with the vast interests dependent upon the wise and economical administration of our inland navigation from the close restrictions which so greatly embarrass them.

The value and importance of opening the whole question, both of the rate of tolls in the canals and of the application of their net revenues, to be freely dealt with in the interests of trade, industry, wealth, and population, instead of keeping it longer subservient to a formal financial policy of debt and credit, which savors more of book-keeping than of enlightened economy, cannot, in my judgment, be over estimated. This freedom of the public action, under the mere motives of the public good, will be quite adequate to meet and accommodate the conflicting policies and discordant views which divide the minds of the people in respect to the ownership and management of our system of inland navigation.

As to what should be adopted as the details of the canal management when this freedom of action in the premises shall have been restored to the State, it would be premature and unprofitable to consider. I have the greatest confidence, however, that the general sense of the community will insist upon an adjustment of the tolls of the canals to the greater interests which build up the wealth and population of the City and State of New-York, rather than to the very narrow and partial computation of the annual income of the mere service of transportation on the canals. Beside the obvious and decisive considerations of a plain political economy which support this policy, and which I need not expand, there is a wholly independent, but quite imperative, motive of *good government* which demands the attention of all who look with a deserved solicitude upon the growing corruption of the times. Just so soon as we reduce the canal administration of this State to the *minimum* of collection and disbursement, necessary to keep open the transit for the burdens of our ever-growing inland trade, we shall have accomplished the greatest and best possible limitation and control over the waste, the corruption and the favoritism which great revenues and great expenditures so surely breed.

I regret that I have been compelled to give so hasty and so brief an expression of my views on the great subject to which you have called my attention, but as they are the result of long reflection upon this branch of the public interests, I have no hesitation in placing them at your service.

I am, very respectfully, your obedient servant,

WM. M. EVARTS.

Mr. Francis D. Moulton, of the Produce Exchange, addressed the meeting in favor of reduction of tolls and the Funding Bill, and presented the following statistics prepared by Mr. Elmore Walker:

GRAIN EXPORTS FROM THE LAKE REGIONS.

STATEMENT showing the Quantities of Flour and Grain sent Eastward from the Lake Regions, comprehending Ohio, Indiana, Michigan, Illinois, Wisconsin, Iowa and Minnesota, and Canada West, for the year 1860:

Eastward Movement—1860.

RECEIVED AT	Flour, bbls.	Wheat, bush.	Corn, bush.	Other Grains, bush.
Wes. Ter. B. & O. RR*	580,750	250,000	127,575	215,065
Wes. Ter. Pa. C. RR*	575,000	500,000	300,000	115,000
Dunkirk	542,765	500,888	644,081	....
Buffalo	1,181,235	18,333,015	11,581,449	1,546,651
Suspension Bridge*	65.374	230,000	22,000	125,000
Oswego	121,399	9,651,564	5,019,400	1,959,642
Ogdensburgh, Dec. 8	381,624	790,178	720,236	48,058
Cape Vincent*	10,390	321,000	25,000	225,000
Montreal	586,497	2,640,957	188,214	846,529
Rochester*	2,750	530,000	....	9 500
Total	4,047,784	40,497,602	18,627,955	5,090,445

* Estimated.

Total Movement Eastward.

YEARS.	Flour, bbls.	Wheat, bush.	Corn, bush.	Other Grains, bush.	Total, bush.
1856	3,865,442	19,505,358	14,282,632	4,592,569	57,707,769
1857	3,397,954	16,763,285	8,779,832	2,256,944	44,789,851
1858	4,499,613	21,843,850	10,495,554	5,035,097	59,872,566
1859	3,760,274	16,865,708	4,423,096	4,264,096	44,354,225
1860	4,047,784	40,497,602	18,627,955	5,090 445	84,454,922
1861	6,533,869	46,384,144	29,524,628	10,656,116	119,264,233
1862	8,483,037	57,220,529	32,098,049	11,286,109	137,669,872
1863	7,782,920	36,513,952	24,955,385	15,983,111	116,367,548
1864	4.687,792	28,705,766	12,387,913	18,452,907	82,985,046
1865	4,920,613	23,301,859	24,401,734	16,943.119	89,249,777

STATEMENT showing the per cent. of Receipts at the Principal Receiving Points, as mentioned in the foregoing movement, for six years, from 1860 to 1865 inclusive:

LOCALITY.	1860.	1861.	1862.	1863.	1864.	1865
Buffalo	47.2	51.5	52 8	55.6	62.4	57.7
Oswego	21.7	15.5	3.3	12.4	12.4	14.5
Montreal	9.2	12.6	13.9	11.8	11.8	9.1
W. Ter. B. & O. R. R.	2.4	3.0	2.9	3.6	1.2	3.9
W. Ter. Pa. C. R. R.	3.9	4.1	4 4	5.2	2.2	3.7
Ogdensburgh	3.5	3.1	3.24	3.42	4.2	4.4
Dunkirk	4.2	3.8	4.1	3.0	3.2	3.7
Suspension Bridge	6 5	5.4	5.1	4.5	1.7	1.7
Cape Vincent	0.8	0.6	0.7	0.35	0.55	0.9
Rochester	0 6	0.1	0.19	0.17	0.25	0.4
Totals	100.0	100.0	100.0	100.0	100.0	100.0
Per cent. of receipts at Buffalo and Oswego.	68.9	67.0	66.1	68.1	74.8	72.2
Leaving for all other points	31.1	33.0	33.9	32.0	25.2	27.8

Of the per cent. of grain receipts at Buffalo, including flour, a very considerable portion has been carried to Eastern markets by the two great through lines of railway, the New-York Central and Erie.

NOTE.—The actual receipts at the Western Termini of the Baltimore and Ohio, and Pennsylvania Central Railways, Suspension Bridge and Rochester, will probably slightly vary the per cent.; but the estimates will very nearly approximate to the actual receipts.

COMPARATIVE AGGREGATE RECEIPTS at Chicago, Milwaukee, Toledo, Detroit and Cleveland, from January 1st, 1869, to January 1st, 1870, inclusive for four years:

	1869.	1868.	1867.	1866.
Flour, bbls...............	5,129,085	4,373,293	3,793,907	4,067,958
Wheat, bush..............	46,012,528	32,105,124	29,565,921	27,987,141
Corn, bush.............	30,171,143	31,619,889	32,198,410	38,228,012
Oats, bush.................	13,454,058	19,563,294	14,205,041	12,757,008
Barley, bush..............	2,302,456	2,685,907	3,014,767	2,294,688
Rye, bush...............	1,384,296	1,790,398	1,721,471	2,356,291
Total Grain, bush........	93,324,481	87,764,612	80,705,610	83,623,140

RECEIPTS OF FLOUR AND GRAIN AT NEW-YORK FOR FOUR YEARS.

	1866.	1867.	1868.	1869.
Flour, bbls.	2,720,835	2,602.892	2,860,726	3,535,716
Wheat, bush...............	5,729,912	9,640,131	12.988,147	23,813,652
Corn, bush.................	22,189,562	14,979,277	19,053,615	11,666,784
Oats, bush.................	8,811,064	8,030,807	10,221,590	8,747,322
Barley, bush..............	5,695,485	2,669,724	2,853,043	3,007,958
Rye, bush.................	1,314,943	765,376	773,351	357,803
Peas, bush................	552,730	668,457	378,423	116,974
Total Grain, bush.........	44,293,696	36,753,772	46,268,169	47,710,493

RECEIPTS OF FLOUR AND GRAIN AT CHICAGO FOR FOUR YEARS.

	1866.	1867.	1868.	1869.
Flour, bbls................	1,847,148	1,720,001	2,092,553	2,234,905
Wheat, bush..............	11,928,753	13,695,244	13,540,250	16,892,818
Corn, bush.................	33,543,061	22,772,715	25,396,523	23,717,505
Oats, bush.................	11,140,264	12,355,006	14,449,486	10,233,866
Barley, bush..............	1,742,652	2,360,984	1,511,219	1,364,372
Rye, bush.................	1,679,541	1,291,821	1,307,461	981,755
Total Grain, bush.........	60,084,271	52,475,770	56,204,939	53,190,316

It will be observed that the Grain Trade of New-York in 1868 was 9,936,770 bushels less than Chicago, and in 1869 was 5,379,823 bushels less. This fact alone should be a warning to the City of New-York.

RECEIPTS OF FLOUR AND GRAIN AT ST. LOUIS FOR FOUR YEARS.

	1866.	1867.	1868.	1869.
Flour, bbls.	1,208,725	944,075	1,036,688	1,026,652
Wheat, bush	4,636,463	3,571,593	4,687,425	6,296,926
Corn, bush.	7,233,274	5,155,460	2,738.515	2,329,588
Oats, bush.	3,567,253	3,445,388	3,210,132	3,059,297
Barley, bush	548,797	702,215	625,340	748,762
Rye, bush	375,417	250,704	364,468	255,946
Total Grain, bush	16,361,604	13,025,360	11,625,880	12,690,019
Flour Manufactured, bbls	818,300	765,298	888,571	1,001,161

THE SHIPMENTS FROM CHICAGO, MILWAUKEE AND TOLEDO, FOR THE YEAR 1869, WERE AS FOLLOWS:

	BY RAIL.	BY WATER.	TOTAL.
Flour, bbls.	2,495,900	1,868,596	4,364,496
Wheat, bush.	5,281,115	28,356,231	33,637,346
Corn, bush.	11,386,490	15,021,791	26,408,281
Oats, bush.	5,247,960	5,166,096	10,414,056
Barley, bush	581.809	29,697	611,506
Rye, bush.	925,644	129,323	1,054,967
Total Grain, bush	23,423,018	48,703,138	72,126,156

The shipments from Western Lake Ports of the United States to Canada, during the past week, have been all by rail, of which there is no published account, although there is a very considerable movement to Montreal, Portland and Ogdensburg, *via* Detroit and Port Huron, over the Grand Trunk and Great Western Railways. The movement through Detroit by rail, during the year 1869, comprised 409,616 bbls. of flour; 237,912 bushels of wheat; 3,118,834 bushels of corn; 1,094,648 bushels of oats; 57,447 bushels of barley, besides large quantities of other classes of freight.

EASTWARD MOVEMENT OF FLOUR AND GRAIN from the Ports of Chicago, Milwaukee, Toledo and Cleveland, from April 17th to and including Nov. 27, 1869, exclusive of Rail Shipments from Cleveland, and including Rail Shipments from Chicago from August 1st only, and destination where known:

TO	FLOUR. Bbls.	WHEAT. Bush.	CORN. Bush.	OATS. Bush.	RYE. Bush.
Buffalo	1,239,468	15,975,337	9,843,330	4,234,094	90,604
Oswego	964	5,107,062	624,749	32,121	27,239
Port Colborne	....	464,854	632,698	....	....
Ogdensburg	223,345	791,441	1,645,168	112,020	....
Cape Vincent	10	203,764	80,555	....	....
Dunkirk	1,682	43,180	30,958	....	....
Erie	49,839	431,013	327,240	69,525	11,400
Saginaw	550	....	38,280	25,343	....
Lake Superior	5,747	42,893	188,469	....	....
Collingwood	....	....	52,018	....	....
Goderich	100	....	104,785	20,713	....
Port Huron	261,589	33,563	1,063,597	68,933	50
Windsor	....	15,029	61,559	....	....
St. Catharines	....	462,855	....	....	....
Kingston	....	4,181,033	75,777	....	....
Prescott	....	....	62,602	....	....
Montreal	13,850	325,885	27,905	....	....
Quebec	....	....	11,200	....	....
Other Ports	71,452	309,795	307,407	414,873	20
By Railroad	653,901	3,489,862	5,820,484	3,146,563	304,360
Total	2,522,497	31,846,093	20,842,275	8,312,659	433,683

The movement to Ogdensburg has been large, as 25 propellers have been running between the Upper Lakes and that port during the past season, besides a considerable number of sailing vessels.

COMPARATIVE RECEIPTS OF FLOUR AND GRAIN AT BUFFALO FOR FOUR YEARS.

	1866.	1867.	1868.	1869.
Flour, bbls	1,313,549	1,417,799	1,524,818	1,666,629
Wheat, bush.	10,515,678	12,298,141	12,647,781	19,335,646
Corn, bush	27,998,542	17,376,378	16,889,952	11,937,131
Oats, bush	10,298,757	10,635,159	11,310,053	5,312,874
Barley, bush	1,672,751	1,798,596	679,241	695,467
Rye, bush	1,193,519	918,330	984,586	125,003
Peas, bush	141,095	152,475	61,512	49,060
Total Grain	51,820,342	43,079,079	42,573,125	37,456,131

COMPARATIVE CANAL SHIPMENTS OF FLOUR AND GRAIN FROM BUFFALO FOR FOUR YEARS.

	1866.	1867.	1868.	1869.
Flour, bbls	52,325	15,465	5,774	51,928
Wheat, bush.	7,772,217	10,109,718	10,369,030	16,363,480
Corn, bush	25,548,596	14,931,312	15,999,136	7,816,960
Oats, bush	8,922,433	9,409,686	10,423,504	3,959,046
Barley, bush	1,301,715	1,206,733	209,218	82,429
Rye, bush	972,647	736,598	633,899	76,792
Total Grain	44,517,608	36,394,527	36,734,787	28,298,707

The difference between the Receipts and Canal Shipments shows a very considerable movement by railroad from Buffalo.

RECEIPTS OF FLOUR AND GRAIN AT ERIE, PA.

	1866.	1867.	1868.	1869.
Flour, bbls	510	400	117,759	153,328
Wheat, bush	....	91,340	424,256	672,291
Corn, bush	13,400	28,551	517,684	637,497
Oats, bush	....	....	314,687	130,286
Barley, bush	....	20,300	52,822	188,091
Rye, bush	....	....	32,239	16 050
Peas, bush	....	....	....	1,074
Total Grain, bush	13,400	140,191	1,341,688	1,645,239
Flour to Wheat, bush	2,550	2,000	588,795	766,640
Total	15,950	142,191	1,930,483	2,411,879

RECEIPTS OF FLOUR AND GRAIN AT OGDENSBURG, N. Y.

YEARS.	Flour, bbls.	Grain, bush.	Total bush. Flour to Wheat.
1869	247,895	2,884,701	....
1868	225,471	2,701,471	....
1867	240,296	2,587,515	....
1866	205,576	2,774,709	....
Total	919,238	10,948,396	15,544,586

RECEIPTS OF FLOUR AND GRAIN AT OSWEGO FOR FOUR YEARS.

	1866.	1867.	1868.	1869.
Flour, bbls	8,309	3,277	1,165	3,526
Wheat, bush	5,517,329	5,279,286	6,970,334	7,789,699
Corn, bush	3,492,207	3,420,784	3,679,346	1,818,170
Oats, bush	356,538	275,514	683,154	62,331
Barley, bush	4,304,803	2,720,334	2,134,310	3,199,747
Rye, bush	572,394	238,177	168,780	334,002
Peas, bush	393,299	669,683	345,603	175,023
Total Grain, bush	14,636,570	12,603,778	13,981,527	13,378,972

SHIPMENTS OF FLOUR AND GRAIN BY CANAL FROM OSWEGO FOR FOUR YEARS.

	1866.	1867.	1868.	1869.
Flour, bbls	151,439	74,001	46,656	68,201
Wheat, bush	2,113,992	2,483,691	3,349,231	4,661,533
Corn, bush	2,835,226	2,740,227	2,911.715	1,613,093
Oats, bush	303,407	266,689	627,440	79,549
Barley. bush	4,066,713	2,590,886	1,916,882	2,749,911
Rye, bush	531,713	241,692	145,964	302,602
Peas, bush	278,885	669,764	346,790	162,682
Total Grain, bush	10,129,936	8,992,949	9,298,022	9,569,370

AND BY RAILROAD.

	1866.	1867.	1868.	1869.
Flour, bbls	450,632	487,435	519,009	492,996
Wheat, bush	106,483	173,757	283,667	173,856
Corn, bush	113,691	237,466	246,596	202,386
Oats, bush	8,583	22,718	16,096	7,428
Barley, bush	13,993	8,246	13,973	84,948
Rye, bush	....	9,676	32	1,826
Peas, bush	2.216	6,915	16,829	3,343
Total Grain, bush	294,966	458,778	577,193	473,787

RECEIPTS OF FLOUR AND GRAIN AT MONTREAL FOR THREE YEARS.

	1867.	1868.	1869.
Flour, bbls	738,518	799,311	984,192
Wheat, bush	2,939,307	2,426,879	7,336,366
Corn, bush	891,605	1,086,204	142,209
Oats, bush	401,498	331,842	34,259
Barley, bush	413,600	268,386	64 925
Rye, bush	146,973	2,797	9,018
Peas, bush	1,812,653	520,408	447,355
Total Grain, bush	6,605,636	4,636,519	8,034,132

EXPORTS FROM MONTREAL FOR THREE YEARS.

	1867.	1868.	1869.
Flour, bbls..................	209,669	510,847	808,386
Wheat, bush................	1,459,622	1,141,573	5,624,887
Corn, bush..................	643 528	735,047	87,274
Oats, bush..................	920,586	864,267	279,231
Barley, bush................	166,038	630,895	147,722
Rye, bush...................	21,918	6	2,069
Peas, bush..................	1,753,748	670,278	510,781
Total Grain, bush........	4,965,440	4,042,066	6,651,964

RECEIPTS OF FLOUR AND GRAIN AT PHILADELPHIA FOR FOUR YEARS.

	1866.	1867.	1868.	1869.
Flour, bbls.................	724,498	508,179	721,810	918,170
Wheat, bush	1,802,010	1.208,892	2,194,160	2,984,600
Corn, bush.................	1,506,305	2,464,125	2,960,127	3,240,140
Oats, bush.................	1,527,470	1,439,940	2,437,680	2,660,570
Barley, bush...............	No report.	No report.	No report.	No report.
Rye, bush..................	....	260,770	762,410	951,465
Total Grain, bush......	4,835,785	5,372,727	8,354,377	9,836,775

RECEIPTS OF FLOUR AND GRAIN AT BALTIMORE FOR FOUR YEARS.

	1866.	1867.	1868.	1869.
Flour, bbls................	1,123,981	888,410	714,760	913,134
Wheat, bush..............	1,359,604	1,792,602	2,293,799	3,249,995
Corn, bush................	4,479,033	5,661,753	4,177,264	3,923,563
Oats, bush................	1,333,510	1,535,449	1,146,175	1,171,424
Rye, bush.................	73,494	125,301	136 270	177,246
Peas, bush................	15,000	10,000	10,000	10,000
Beans, bush..............	30,000	30,000	3,000	40,000
Total Grain, bush......	8,562,228	7,793,508	9,155,105	7,300,641

RECEIPTS OF FLOUR AND GRAIN AT BOSTON FOR FOUR YEARS.

	1866.	1867.	1868.	1869.
Flour, bbls..................	1,504,253	1,402,826	1,467,681	1,479,975
Wheat, bush...	16,537	159,421	165,240	369,059
Corn, bush.......	2,157,292	2,361,313	2,470,148	2,343,840
Oats, bush.................	1,219,717	1,411,176	1,294,446	1,400,412
Barley, bush................	190,658	317,911	212,167	316,871
Rye, bush..................	27,864	24,311	27,714	32,992
Total Grain, bush.......	3,622,068	4,274,132	4,169,715	4,463,174

RECAPITULATION, taking the Flour and Grain Receipts (including all kinds of Grain) at the five Lake Ports, including Chicago, Milwaukee, Toledo, Detroit and Cleveland, and estimating each barrel of flour equal to five bushels of wheat, the sum total of receipts, in bushels, for each undermentioned year is as follows :

	1866.	1867.	1868.	1869.
Connecticut*...........	7,500,000	8,500,000	8,750,000	9,000,000
Five Lake Ports......	89,584,346	103,462,930	109,631,077	118,969,906
St. Louis	22,405,229	17,745,735	16,809,320	17,824,779
Total..............	119,489,575	129,708,665	135,190,397	145,794,685

*Estimated.

	1866.	1867.	1868.	1869.
New York Receipts.....	57,897,871	49,768,232	60,571,799	65,389,073
Montreal..............	10,100,881	10,298,226	8,588,065	12,955,092
Boston............. .	11,143,333	11,288,262	11,508,120	11,863,049
Philadelphia...........	8,458,275	7,913,622	11,963,427	14,427,625
Baltimore.	14,181,133	12,235,558	12,728,905	11,866,311
Ogdensburg...........	3,802,589	3,788,995	3,828,826	4,124,176
New Orleans*	10,500,000	11,000,000	11,500,000	12,500,000
Total..............	58,186,211	56,524,663	60,117,343	67,736,253

*Estimated, 1865.

The Receipts at Chicago and New-York compare as follows :

Chicago..............	69,319,996	61,075,775	66,667,704	64,364,841
New-York.............	57,897,871	49,768,232	60,571,799	65,389,073

NAMES OF CANALS.	Length in Miles.	Income from Tolls to and including September 30th, 1866.	Interest on Income from Tolls to September 30th, 1866.	Aggregate Income and Interest on same to September 30th, 1866.	Cost of Construction, Enlargement, Extension and Improvement	Cost of Repairs, Maintenance and Collection of Revenues.	Aggregate of Construction, Enlargement, Extension, Maintenance and Collection of Revenues.	Interest on Cost of Construction and other Disbursements.	Aggregate Cost of Canals, including Maintenance and Interest on same.	Canals that had a Debit Balance September 30th, 1866, Amount of Same.	Canals that had a Credit Balance September 30th, 1866.
Erie Canal	350½	$87,522,833 23	$95,335,082 64	$182,857,915 87	$43,865,482 59	$14,513,528 72	$58,379,014 31	$83,042,410 92	$141,421,425 23		$41,436,490 64
Champlain	66¾	4,593,908 44	5,003,955 26	9,597,863 70	2,152,751 60	3,039,092 58	5,191,841 18	7,386,952 55	12,578,793 73	$2,980,930 03	
Oswego	38	2,563,639 48	1,852,327 53	4,415,957 01	3,490,949 24	1,812,571 42	5,303,520 66	4,910,029 43	10,213,550 09	5,797,573 08	
Cayuga and Seneca	24¾	805,517 96	934,531 46	1,740,049 42	1,520,542 59	620,050 22	2,140,592 81	2,121,346 94	4,261,939 75	2,521,890 33	
Chemung	39	455,774 22	429,042 76	884,816 98	1,273,261 86	1,139,770 30	2,413,032 16	2,606,403 96	5,019,436 12	4,134,619 14	
Crooked Lake	8	42,373 90	51,996 97	94,340 87	333,287 27	258,282 78	591,570 05	772,076 12	1,363,646 17	1,269,305 30	
Chenango	97	614,009 59	590,031 26	1,204,040 85	2,782,124 19	970,169 49	3,752,293 68	5,865,059 77	9,617,353 45	8,413,312 60	
Black River	99¾	114,576 02	48,324 87	162,900 89	3,224,779 55	455,011 36	3,669,790 91	4,724,535 70	8,394,326 61	8,231,425 72	
Genessee Valley	124¾	631,870 58	526,214 85	1,158,085 43	5,827,813 72	1,405,342 66	7,233,156 38	9,180,166 58	16,413,322 96	15,255,237 53	
Oneida Lake	7	65,189 51	57,880 33	123,060 84	64,837 68	123,234 92	188,072 60	207,442 00	395,514 60	272,453 76	
Baldwinsville	1	1,261 48	979 27	2,240 75	23,556 14	25,035 26	48,591 40	23,751 94	72,343 34	70,102 59	
Oneida River Imp't Seneca River Towing Path	5 5¾	204,288 91 5,251 69	158,439 27 3,096 41	362,728 18 8,348 10	146,994 32 1,458 33	25,005 50 19 54	171,999 82 1,507 87	164,379 07 572 07	336,378 59 2,079 94		26,349 59 6,263 16
Cayuga Inlet		4,596 96	2,569 23	7,166 19	2,968 16		2,968 16	423 61	3,391 77		3,774 42
Total	*900	$97,625,072 97	$104,994,412 11	$202,619,515 08	$64,710,836 94	$24,377,114 75	$89,087,951 69	$121,005,550 66	$210,093,502 35	$48,946,870 08	$41,472,877 81

* With feeders and basins 900 miles long.

After addresses from Hon. Erastus Brooks, Hon. Elijah Ward, Nathaniel Sands. Esq., and others, the following resolutions were unanimously adopted:

RESOLUTIONS.

Whereas, The people of the State of New-York have unanimously demanded of their representatives such a system of management of, and such legislation concerning, the New-York State canals as will increase their trade and their facilities for transportation; and several proposed laws have been introduced in the Legislature, or will be introduced, aiming to secure those most desirable ends, being: 1. An Act to abolish the Contracting Board and the system of repairing the canals by contract. 2. An Act to abolish the office of Canal Appraisers, and to establish in lieu thereof a Court of Claims with competent judges. 3. A resolution to concur with the Canal Board in the reduction of tolls on the canals, all of which this meeting heartily approves; and whereas, measures are in contemplation whereby the balance of the State debt heretofore provided for out of the tolls, may be funded, so as to relieve the canals from the burden of paying such debt, and so lead to an important reduction in tolls, and finally in free transportation; therefore, be it

Resolved, That this meeting is of opinion that it is of the most pressing necessity that the Legislature and the Canal Board should take such measures as will provide for a reduction of the canal tolls; that while the Constitution has directed annual appropriations from the canal revenues to be applied to the extinguishment of certain State debts, and the reduction of tolls may at first reduce the revenues below such appropriation, it is necessary, in order to avoid a direct annual tax for the deficiency, to provide other means for such extinguishment.

Resolved, That the proposed bill, presented to this meeting, and indorsed by the Hon. I. T. Hatch, the Hon. John K. Porter, the Hon. George F. Comstock, the Hon. John Ganson, and the Hon. William M. Evarts, which provides for funding the said State debts and extending their payment over 18 years, fully meets all the necessities of the case, and will, if passed, accomplish the desired end, viz.: relieve the people from a heavy annual tax, provide for the payment of the State debts, and free the trade of the canals from the burden of the present excessive tolls.

Resolved, That this proposed Funding Bill recommends itself to the approval of the Legislature and the whole people of the State, and should become a law; that the Representatives in Senate and Assembly be urged to pass the bill and submit it to the electors at the next general election.

Resolved, That the future prosperity of our State depends largely on the adoption of this comprehensive plan of relieving and benefiting the canals and their trade, and as a wise and statesmanlike measure.

Resolved, That the State Central Committee of the Commercial Union, present these resolutions and an Act or Acts in conformity therewith to the Legislature.

JOSEPH F. DALY,
Secretary.

Printed in Poland
by Amazon Fulfillment
Poland Sp. z o.o., Wrocław

68426422R00066